Science on the Shores and Banks

by Elizabeth K. Cooper
(available in hard-cover editions)

SCIENCE IN YOUR OWN BACK YARD
DISCOVERING CHEMISTRY
SCIENCE ON THE SHORES AND BANKS
SILKWORMS AND SCIENCE: *The Story of Silk*
INSECTS AND PLANTS: *The Amazing Partnership*
AND EVERYTHING NICE: *The Story of*
Sugar, Spice, and Flavoring

MINERALS: *Their Identification, Uses,*
and How to Collect Them
(with Herbert S. Zim)

(available in a Voyager paperback edition)

SCIENCE IN YOUR OWN BACK YARD

SCIENCE
ON THE
SHORES
AND
BANKS

ELIZABETH K. COOPER

with illustrations by the author

A VOYAGER BOOK

HARCOURT, BRACE & WORLD, INC., NEW YORK

To Aunt Rose and Aunt Bertha, who
first introduced me to the beach
when I was very young

CONTENTS

Science on the Shores and Banks

ONE

Exploring the Water's Edge

Wherever a body of water meets the land, you can discover a rich and exciting field for science. There is much to observe because you really have three separate worlds right there at arm's reach. First, you have the water world of plants and animals that cannot live except in the water. A fish will drown if you hold it too long in the air. It gets its oxygen from the water. Its body is beautifully formed for living and moving in its water environment. You have probably heard the saying, "As helpless as a fish out of water" — and that is helpless, indeed! Man and some other animals can learn to swim in water, but a fish cannot learn to swim in the air. Plants and animals that live in water have special features that enable them to thrive only in their native surroundings. There are plants without roots or leaves or flowers, living and drifting endlessly in the sea. There are animals that can regrow parts of their bodies that have been cut off and even, when cut into several pieces, grow each piece into a complete new body. There are animals that look and live like plants, and plants that are never green. There are animals that move on a single foot, and some that cannot move at all. Seaweed and pondweed and oysters and starfish and minnows and hydra are only a few of the living things that are perfectly at home in their water world.

The second life-area is on the bank or shore itself. It is the world of air and sun and dry land. This is the environment for flowers and trees and land birds and people and many other kinds of animals, large and small. The plants and animals of this air world cannot live long under water. You may be able to swim under water for a short time by holding your breath, but there is no way in which you, as a typical land animal, can live without getting oxygen from the air.

The third special area is the in-between world of air and water, the world of plants and animals that need both in order to live. There you will find insects that dive under water and insects that can walk on the surface without getting their feet wet. You can find the water boatman, which lives and feeds in the waters of ponds and quiet streams. But it must breathe air in order to live. Frogs and toads and other amphibians begin their lives as fishlike creatures, getting oxygen directly from the water. For the rest of their lives they are air breathers

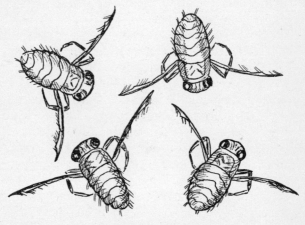

Water boatmen

on the land or they dive into the water and come up every so often for a breath of air. There are many kinds of shore birds that depend upon water for food and upon the air world for everything else. They breathe air and fly through it and then paddle or float on the top of the water or even dive down below the surface to catch a seafood dinner. There are plants, too, like cattails and bulrushes, that need to have both water and air. Their roots grow in the mud deep below the water's surface, and their stems and blades and flowers extend up into the air and sunshine.

Wherever you go to explore the water's edge, there are enough science adventures to keep you busy for a week, a year, or for your entire life, depending on how much you want to find out about the interesting plants and animals along the shores and banks. There are things for a scientist to observe, explore, collect, and experiment with. Here's one way to begin.

First of all, just look around you. Practice sitting quietly until you can see the smallest motion near you. It may be some sand fleas tumbling out of a clump of damp seaweed and scurrying to bury themselves in the sand. Or, if you are beside a pond, it may be a water strider skating across the surface,

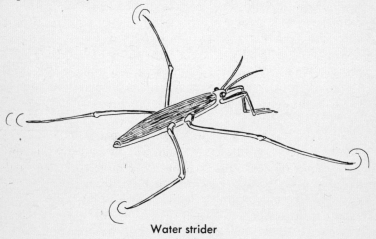

Water strider

his six slender legs ending in delicate feet that make dimples in the water as he moves. Or you may see a dragonfly with wings like cellophane hovering and darting above the reeds, or a crayfish under the water scooting backward to a safe place under some rocks.

Try to learn the art of listening, too. Close your eyes and find out what sounds there are around you and what each sound means. At first you may hear only the sound of the water itself. It may be the slow and regular breaking of waves against the shore. Or you may be hearing the bubbling and gurgling of a stream moving over the rocks, or perhaps the gentle lapping of a quiet lake against its banks. Suddenly you may hear a loud plop as a frog drops from an overhanging tree root into a pool. You may hear a double splash as a fish jumps out of the water and right back in again. Perhaps you can hear the faint buzzing of insects, or the flap-flap of wings and the cry of a sea bird as it dives suddenly toward the water. What special sounds can you hear, and how many of them can you identify?

Explore with your nose, too, for there are many unusual smells around the water's edge. There is the fresh, clean smell of wind blowing across a clear lake. Or the acid-sharp smell of wet willows and alder trees that grow beside a stream. There is the salty tang of the ocean, mingled at times with just a hint of the smell of dead fish. There are special smells wherever you are — the delicate smells of plant and animal life at the edge of the water, and the heavier smells of plant and animal death as the once living tissue softens, breaks apart, and is slowly intermingled with the water.

Now, for a close look, find a shallow place and put your face as close to the water as you can without actually touching it. You may be able to stretch out on a large rock, feet high and head low, and peer down into the water. Or lie on the bank of a stream with your head hanging over the water's edge. Or just wade in where the water is no more than two feet deep, bend over, and see what you can see. Try not to move. Do you see any moving creatures? Watch for swimming and diving insects, tiny fish, tadpoles, snails, turtles, crabs, and any other creatures that may live in these waters. Look also for the slippery, slimy algae growing on rocks and driftwood. You may discover some ribbon-like blades of eelgrass growing from a clump of roots in the mud, or the feathery strands of waterweed waving gently in the current. Or, at the edge of the sea, you may see several kinds of seaweed, perhaps a sheet of light green sea lettuce, a rope of floating brown sargassum, or a spray of rockweed, which is kept afloat by balloon-like air bladders. If it is a sunny day and the glare of the sun on the water begins to tire your eyes, try to make a shadow on the water. Then look through your own shadow and see what else you can discover. Strange plants, interesting insects, and amazing animals of many kinds — you should be able to discover some of them just by using your own powers of observation.

You may also find some interesting nonliving things to observe and collect and experiment with. Look for empty shells of different sizes, colors, and kinds. You may discover, too, some pieces of smooth driftwood, worn into graceful shapes or festooned with green algae or encrusted with shell-covered animals.

As you gaze down into this water world, think of it as an environment for living things. Plants and animals, water and rocks, and the light that filters down from the sun — all have effects upon each other. Among the animals, there is a ceaseless struggle to catch something to eat — and to avoid being caught and eaten. But nearly every living thing you see can provide food for some other living thing. Tiny tadpoles eat algae and other water plants; bigger tadpoles and large insects eat the little tadpoles; fish and frogs eat insects; and the smaller fish are eaten by the larger fish. Yet there are almost always enough of each kind of creature left to keep the waters well stocked. Nature has provided with great abundance in order that this eat-and-be-eaten life can continue. As you watch the struggle for existence in the water world, you will discover some interesting relationships among the creatures who live and die there.

After you have begun to look at and listen to and think about some of the things that are happening at the water's edge, perhaps you will want to explore further, using some of the methods and materials suggested in the next chapter. You can work alone or with friends, boys or girls of almost any age. You may find new interests and hobbies that will last for many years. And, who knows, you may even discover some special science field that is important enough to you to become your life's work. Whatever you find in your exploring at the water's edge, you are sure to have the fun of adventure and the thrill of discovery.

TWO

Scientific Equipment and Methods

After you have spent some time just looking, listening, and sniffing at the water's edge, you will be ready to begin your scientific exploring. In order to work in a systematic and effective way, you will need to have the proper tools and equipment. Some of these things you may have at home or at school. Some you may be able to borrow or buy. Most of them, however, you can make or assemble from odds and ends found in the kitchen, the tool shed, and the rubbish barrel. Remember that these are only *suggestions* of things that may be useful to you. For your particular exploring projects, you will probably need only a few of the items listed here.

Equipment to Help You Observe
　Hand-lens magnifying glass for all careful observing
　Low-power microscope for observing life in drops of
　　water
　A glass dish for looking down into the water

Tools for Collecting Specimens
　Garden trowel
　Putty knife
　Large spading fork
　Small hand fork or rake
　Kitchen strainer, 4″ to 5″ across
　Tin cans
　Spoons
　Nylon water net

Containers for Live Specimens
　Small glass jars with screw tops, the kind used for peanut
　　butter and mayonnaise

Metal or plastic window screening
Tank aquarium; fish globe; large wide-mouthed pickle
    jar, or other large glass containers
Glass-walled or wire-screen terrarium
Metal pail
Cake pan
Pie tins
Dishpan
Plastic jars and dishes

Materials for Making and Keeping Collections of
Nonliving Things
    Cardboard egg cartons
    Cigar boxes with cardboard dividers
    Glass or clear plastic pill bottles with caps
    Sheets of heavy white paper for mounting seaweed and
        other water-plant specimens
    Traylike cardboard boxes that hosiery comes in
    Other shallow cardboard boxes

Materials for Recording Things
    Notebook and pencil
    Sketch pad and crayons or paints
    Camera and film
    Labels for permanent collections
    Waterproof ink and pen for writing labels
    Scotch tape
    Scrapbook

Miscellaneous Supplies
    Small stiff scrubbing brush
    Sandpaper
    Scissors
    Pocket knife
    Wire
    Stapler
    Old pots and pans
    Old newspapers
    Old cardboard boxes

Modeling clay
Plaster of Paris

Using some of the materials listed above, you can make some simple but useful tools and equipment. Here are a few ideas to get you started.

Make a scoop for water creatures by fastening an ordinary kitchen strainer to a long handle. For the handle, use a dowel rod, a broom handle, or a yardstick. Use wire or very strong twine to tie the short handle of the strainer to the long rod or

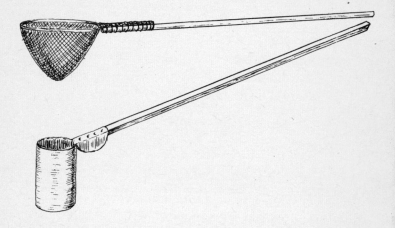

stick. Another kind of scoop can be made from a small tin can. Punch holes with a large nail or an ice pick in the bottom of a frozen-juice can. Bend the top of the can backward and nail it to a long, flat handle. Use the tin-can scoop when you want to dredge up mud or sand from the bottom of a body of water.

A handy net to use for dragging through the water can be made from a nylon stocking. Use a ladies' stocking, one that has no wide runs in it. Spread open the top and sew it around a wooden hoop, the kind sold in dime stores as embroidery hoops. Next, take two pieces of strong, heavy cord, each about a foot long. Poke four holes in the stocking right next to the hoop. Think of the hoop as the face of a clock, and punch the holes at twelve o'clock, three o'clock, six o'clock, and nine o'clock. Tie one end of one cord in the twelve-o'clock hole and the opposite end in the six-o'clock hole. Tie one end of the other cord in the three-o'clock hole and the opposite end in the nine-o'clock hole. Then, hold up your net by the two loops of cord. Where the cords cross, tie them together with a long, strong cord. Use the long cord to hold or to tie to a boat when you drag your nylon net through the water.

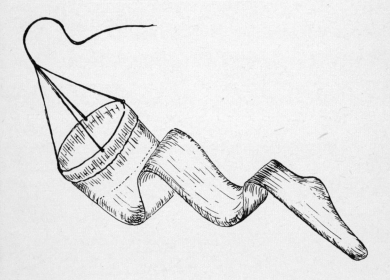

Use glass jars of all sizes as containers for live water creatures. Make covers for the jars by bending pieces of wire or plastic window screening to fit over the open tops. Cheesecloth or mosquito netting can also be used to cover open jars. If cloth is used, you will have to tie it around the jar neck with a string or fasten it with a strong rubber band.

A large, beautiful, and inexpensive aquarium can be made from a five-gallon water bottle. This is the way to do it. Lay the bottle on its side. Make a hollow-square wooden frame for it to rest on. This can be made of four one-half-by-one-inch strips. This light frame will keep the bottle from rolling. If the bottle has a cork, pound the cork in tightly so that it is completely watertight. If it is a screw-cap bottle, make sure that the cap will not leak. You may wish to seal the cork or the cap by covering it with hot sealing wax. However, this is not necessary if you are sure that water cannot leak out.

Your next step is to go to a tombstone cutter and have one side of the bottle sandblasted off. This will cost very little, and the man who does the job will see to it that the cut edges of the bottle are sandblasted smooth. Your aquarium will then be ready to use. Large water bottles are often made of lovely blue-green glass, which makes a very real-looking setting for underwater gardens.

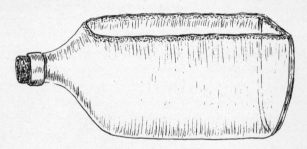

Small aquariums can be made in any glass containers that are wide-mouthed. A container with a small opening does not allow enough oxygen to reach the water's surface. If you are trying to keep water specimens for any length of time, do not put them into a narrow-necked bowl or jar filled to the top with water. If you use such a vessel, fill it only to the widest part. This will leave a large area of surface water for the air to reach.

As you get on with your exploring, you will invent new uses for old materials. You will discover new ways of taking care of the particular collections and experiments that interest you most.

In order to work scientifically, you will want to use not only proper tools and equipment but also proper ways of working. Scientists usually follow definite steps when they are trying to find out about something. They use what is called a scientific method. Here is an outline of some steps you might like to follow in order to work in a scientific way.

FIRST, CHOOSE A PROBLEM. Think about what you want to discover. Decide on a question you want to have answered. You may have some questions like the following ones.

Are all worms alike?

Why do some starfish have one short arm?

How long does it take for a tadpole to grow into a frog?

Are dragonflies dangerous?

Can a crab live out of water?

SECOND, GATHER INFORMATION. Use as many ways as possible to collect information about the subject of your problem. Here are some ways in which you can get information.

Make observations

Collect samples or live specimens

Look at pictures

Go to see exhibits in museums

Read about things in books

Ask people who know something about the subject

THIRD, MAKE TESTS OR EXPERIMENTS. Try to find answers to your questions by trying things out. Use measurements when you can. Experiment in ways like the following.

Measure how fast something grows

Try feeding different kinds of food to animals you are studying

Test a creature's senses with a flashlight, strong perfume on a wad of cotton, raw liver, and a bell

Try growing water plants in sunshine and in shade

Saw shells in half

FOURTH, KEEP RECORDS OF THINGS YOU SEE AND DO. Try some of these different ways of recording your observations and experiments.

Keep a diary, listing the things you see and do on various days

Make black and white sketches, diagrams, and charts

Make colored drawings and water-color paintings from nature

Take photographs and keep them in an album

Cut out pictures and articles from magazines and newspapers and paste them in a scrapbook

FIFTH, DECIDE ON A POSSIBLE ANSWER TO YOUR ORIGINAL PROBLEM. Your answer should be based on all the information you have gathered on the subejct.

What did your observations show?

What did your experiments suggest?

What is the opinion of experts?

What do the books say?

Have you found any differences of opinion on the subject?

What is YOUR opinion?

Why?

SIXTH, CHECK AND RECHECK YOUR CONCLUSION BY MORE OBSERVATIONS, READING, AND EXPERIMENTING. It is important to realize that even after you have gone through all of these steps, the answers you discover may be true for only a certain time and under certain conditions. Scientists often remind us that there are few if any answers that are true for ever and ever. The earth and all that is in it, on it, and around it is continuously changing. As things change, and as more things are discovered, the answers to problems may change, too. Few questions have a single simple answer. While you are searching for answers, you will be making many discoveries. You will also be getting practical experience in using scientific methods.

THREE

Insects of the Water World

The first animal life you are likely to notice as you begin to explore is the flitting, darting, whirling, diving life of insects. Of all the water animals that are big enough for you to see, most of them are insects. You can find them in quiet ponds, in flowing streams, in roadside ditches, and in lakes that are edged with green rushes. Any body of fresh water with green plants growing in or around it will have many kinds of insects living among the leaves, stems, and roots.

As you look down into the water through a tangle of green plants, you will see a jungle in which strange animals live and die. Some of these animals seem frightening and ugly. Others look graceful and lovely. All of them are wonderfully formed for the jobs they have to do — hunt food, capture prey, escape enemies, find mates, lay eggs, and finally die and become part of the earth's crust.

As you watch several small creatures diving through the water or darting across the surface, you may wonder whether they are insects or some other kinds of water animals. It is not always easy to tell which are insects. Here are some clues to help you identify them.

First of all, water insects have the same general features as all insects. Every adult is a six-legged animal with a body that is in three parts. Its body has no bones but is protected by a hard coating or shell. Also, nearly every adult insect has two pairs of wings. And nearly every insect, no matter where it lives, passes through three or four separate stages during its lifetime.

The four-stage insects lay eggs that hatch into larvae, which are little wormlike creatures. The larvae eat and grow until

23

they are ready for the third stage. Then they build themselves cocoons in which they rest quietly. In this stage they are called pupae. During the pupa stage, their bodies gradually change into adult forms. At the end of the pupa stage, the insects break out of their cocoons and are ready to fly off as winged adults.

The three-stage insects lay eggs, too. But their eggs hatch into nymphs or naiads, which are quite different from worm-like larvae. They are called nymphs or naiads after the water sprites in Greek and Roman myths. The baby water insects can breathe, eat, and grow under the water. In time, the nymphs or naiads climb out of their water world, split their skins, and emerge as winged, air-breathing insects. They are the adults that will return to the water when the time comes to mate and lay their eggs. Such insects grow from egg to nymph or naiad and to adult, while other insects change from egg to larva to pupa and then to adult. It is in the adult stage that insects are easily recognized, mainly by their six legs, three-part bodies, and two pairs of wings.

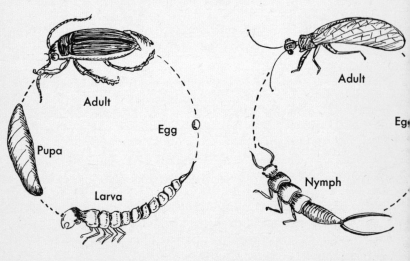

Adult

Pupa

Egg

Larva

Water beetle
A four-stage insect

Adult

Eg

Nymph

Stone fly
A three-stage insect

How many different kinds of adult insects can you spot as you explore the water's edge? Watch for them flying among the water weeds on the shore, hiding in the blossoms of water lilies, hopping and crawling among the rocks, skating over the surface of the water, diving beneath the surface, and clinging to the underwater stems of plants. Watch a single insect for a long time and try to figure out what it is doing. Chances are that it is busy getting food to eat or oxygen to breathe.

Insects, like all other animals, need oxygen. Most water insects, in the adult stage, breathe oxygen from the air. Some of them take in air through breathing tubes. When they go beneath the surface, they hold their breathing tubes above the water like little snorkels. Others capture air under their wings or carry bubbles of air on the fine hairs on the undersides of their bodies. The air passes into their bodies through little breathing holes in their sides.

Some water insects, especially in the nymph or naiad stage, can get oxygen directly from the water just as fish can do. They draw water in through special openings in their bodies, pass the water through gills, which take the oxygen out of the water, and then expel the water. Animals that can get their oxygen right from the water do not need to come to the surface to breathe unless something happens to make the water lose its oxygen.

There are several ways in which oxygen gets into water in the first place. All along the surface of the water, tiny amounts of air gradually become dissolved in the water. There is more dissolved air near the top of the water than near the bottom. Wherever there are falls or rapids or swiftly rushing streams, a great deal of air is dashed or beaten into the water, just as you can beat air into egg whites with an egg beater. The fish, insects, and other animals that live in such streams are the ones that need a great deal of oxygen from the water. The animals living in swamps, marshes, ponds, and other quiet waters are ones needing less oxygen. But they all need some oxygen.

Every body of water in which green plants grow gets some oxygen from the plants. As the plants use the sun's energy in manufacturing food, they give off oxygen. This oxygen dissolves in the water and makes it possible for the water breathers to live where the green plants grow.

If you are doing your exploring beside a pond or stream or any other body of fresh water, you should be able to discover some of the interesting water insects described below. When you spot them, watch them carefully and find out how they behave in their natural homes. Later, you may want to capture some specimens and keep them for a while so that you can observe them more closely and use them in some simple experiments. Here are the ones to watch for.

WATER STRIDERS. You will find these long-legged insects walking on the surface of quiet water. They look like daddy longlegs or other long-legged spiders. Some people call them "water spiders," but spiders, which are not insects at all, have eight legs. Water striders, like other insects, have only six legs. Watch a water strider as it moves daintily on top of the water. It looks as though it were skating on clear ice. As each of its delicate legs touches the water, it makes a tiny dent in the surface. Its feet do not pierce the film of water.

You can do an experiment at home to show how the strider's legs can rest on the water without breaking through and sinking. Fill a teacup with water. Let the water stand until it is perfectly still. Then take an ordinary needle and very, very carefully lower it horizontally onto the surface of the water. The needle will float. This is because the water forms a tight film where it meets the air. The water film is strong enough to hold up the needle and to support the delicate steps of the water strider.

The body of a water strider is covered with oily hairs. If it gets wet, it will not drown because the hairs will hold enough air bubbles to keep its light body afloat. Watch a water strider as it moves across the water. It uses its middle pair of legs to push itself along. Its front legs are held ready to catch any little insect that happens to land in its path. Its front legs grab the prey and carry it to its mouth. As the strider does this, the back pair of legs help to balance its long, slim body. It has a sharp beak, which it uses to kill its prey. It eats the soft parts and throws the rest away. Then it is ready to stride on and look for another snack.

Water striders lay their eggs on plants that grow in the water, or on the undersides of floating leaves. During the winter they go to sleep under dead leaves at the edge of the water. The cold weather slows them down, and they need very little oxygen or food till warm days come again in the spring.

Water striders are one of the few kinds of insects that live on the sea as well as on fresh water. There is a kind of water strider that lives among the floating seaweed hundreds of miles from land.

BACK SWIMMER. As its name suggests, the back swimmer swims upside down. Its back is shaped like a little boat, one-fourth to one-half an inch long. It uses its hind legs like a pair of oars. It appears white or silvery in the water. This is because its underside, which is up when it is swimming, is covered with tiny bubbles of air. This is its way of carrying its own supply of air. When it dives beneath the surface, the air goes into the breathing holes on its body. It usually carries so much air that it has a hard time staying under water. When it wants to stay under for a while, it has to hold onto something under the water. And as soon as it lets go, up it comes again. Like water striders, back swimmers have pointed beaks for killing their prey and sucking out the body juices.

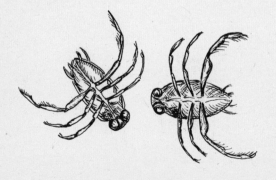

Back swimmers

WATER BOATMEN. If you find some back swimmers, you may discover some other little insects that look very much like them. These are the water boatmen. They skim across the surface film of the water like tiny boats, using their hair-fringed middle pair of legs as oars. Unlike the back swimmers, the boatmen travel right side up. Their little oval bodies are one-fourth to one-half an inch long, and they move swiftly across the water in irregular, jerky patterns. They can carry bubbles of air down with them when they go beneath the surface. Some boatmen can fly well, but they do most of their flying by night. In the daytime they usually stay on and in the water, hunting for smaller insects, which they pierce with their sharp beaks in order to suck out the body fluids.

GIANT WATER BUGS. The largest and most vicious of the water insects you are likely to see are the giant water bugs. They are usually about two inches long. Some have been found as long as three inches. They breathe air through a tube in their tails as they hang head down in the water hunting for tadpoles and other small water creatures. They eat only living things, which they attack with their fierce beaks. They then suck out the soft parts and discard the skin, shell, or other hard parts.

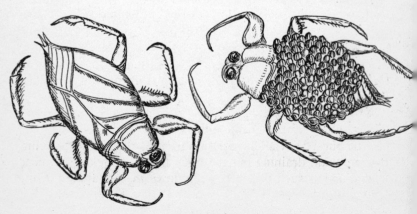

Giant water bugs

When they dive, water bugs carry bubbles of air under their wings. When this air is used up, they return to the surface and breathe in fresh air through the breathing tube in their tails. Giant water bugs move about easily by pushing with their strong back legs. They are found in dark, shadowy places in quiet waters. They do not like the sunlight.

The bite of a giant water bug is not poisonous to human beings, but it can be very painful and usually causes a sore swelling. It is not an insect to be played with or to be caught in your bare hands.

Some female water bugs lay their eggs on the leaves of pond plants. But many of the females have a more unusual way of providing for their eggs. They lay them on the backs of the male water bugs, fastened on tightly in a sack, which protects the eggs. The eggs look like a bunch of fat little seeds. They stay on the father's back for about ten days until they hatch into little water-bug nymphs. Once the eggs have hatched, the sack with its empty egg cases falls off the father's back. The little nymphs move about on their own, and as they grow, they shed their skins about six times until they become adults.

WATER SCORPIONS. Another meat-eating insect is the water scorpion, which looks something like the praying mantis. Its body is very long, four or five inches, and very thin. It breathes air through a tube more than an inch long that extends out from its tail. It holds this breathing tube out of the water like a little snorkel. Water scorpions stalk their prey among the water plants, catch them with a swift grasp of their forelegs, pierce them with their sharp beaks, and draw out the soft parts for food.

You have probably noticed that all of the water insects mentioned so far have the same kinds of feeding habits. They are all true bugs. They all have mouth parts like beaks for piercing live prey and draining out the body fluids. They are all meat eaters, and as such they help keep down the population of insects and other small water creatures. If you watch them for any length of time, you will discover that they even help reduce the population of their own kind. They do not seem to hesitate to eat each other. Any creature smaller than itself seems to be a fair meal for one of the water bugs.

WATER BEETLES. Water beetles are different from water bugs in several ways. First of all, like all true beetles, they have a pair of hard outer wings over a pair of soft flying wings. Like the bugs, the water beetles are meat eaters, but their mouth parts have regular jaws with which they bite and chew. They hunt for nymphs, tiny fish, and other small water creatures, dive after them, and tear them apart with their strong jaws.

Whirligig beetles swim in circles, whirl around on top of the water, dive easily, and can also fly. They hibernate under the water in winter and rise to the surface as the water warms in the spring. Their eyes are in two parts, a lower part for looking under the water and an upper part for looking above, into the air.

Diving water beetles are harder to find than their whirligig cousins. They hang head down, breathing through their tails. They carry a bubble of air down with them when they dive.

The largest of all the water beetles is the *water scavenger*, which is sometimes over three inches long. It is a good insect to keep by itself in a small aquarium because it will eat bits of raw meat and seems to do well in captivity.

All of the water beetles look purple, green, or even red as the sun shines on their hard backs. Their undersides seem silvery because of the tiny air bubbles they carry close to their bodies.

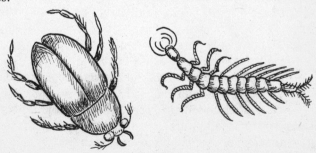

Beetle and larva

DRAGONFLIES. Probably the best hunter of the insect world is the dragonfly. It can outfly almost any other insect. It has been known to fly as fast as a mile a minute. It spots its prey in the air, overtakes it, grasps it with its strong, bristly legs, and eats it with its powerful jaws — all while flying swiftly through the air. Dragonflies have lovely fairy-like wings of veined gauze and a long, needle-thin body. They have been called "darning needles" and "ear-sewers," and some people are afraid of them. They are, indeed, very dangerous creatures, but only to other insects. As far as we are concerned, dragonflies are helpful friends. They are great eaters, and their favorite food seems to be mosquitoes and other small flies that are harmful or annoying to people.

Dragonflies in their flying (adult) stage are, of course, often found far from the water. But before reaching this stage, all dragonflies live in water. The mother dragonfly lays its eggs on the leaves of water plants or just drops them into the water. The eggs hatch into nymphs, which are true water animals. They get oxygen from the water and prey upon all smaller water creatures for food.

A dragonfly nymph has a special kind of lower lip, which can be flipped out in a flash to extend nearly as long as the nymph's body. At the end of this lip are jawlike parts, which grasp mosquito larvae, tiny fish, or other small water creatures. The nymph, like the adult, has a large appetite. It can eat its own weight in a single meal. Most of the time, a nymph lies quietly on the bottom of a pond or stream, half covered with mud or sand, watching and waiting for food to pass within striking distance of its deadly lower lip. When it moves, it is jet-propelled by means of water it takes in and forces out through a hole on its underside.

A dragonfly stays in the nymph stage for a year or more until, on some spring or summer day, the time comes for it to leave its water world. Some inner force or rhythm makes it climb out of the water, usually by moving up the stem of a water plant. Then, above the water for the first time in its life, the nymph fastens its legs to the plant. This holds it secure while its back splits open. Gradually, the adult dragonfly

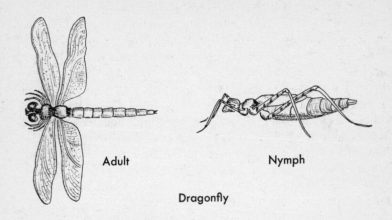

Adult   Nymph

Dragonfly

emerges from its shell, its gossamer wings damp and folded and crumpled. It stretches and spreads its wings, dries them in the sun or in the warm air, and flies away.

DAMSEL FLIES. A damsel fly looks very much like a dragonfly. You can tell them apart, however, by noticing several ways in which they are different. Damsel flies are smaller than dragonflies. And when a damsel fly rests on a leaf or stem, it folds its wings. A dragonfly keeps its wings outstretched like airplane wings even while resting.

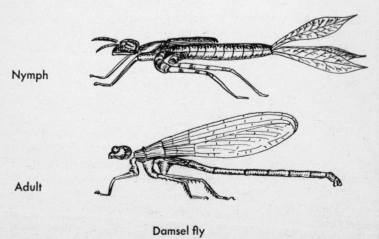

Nymph

Adult

Damsel fly

The young damsel flies pass through a nymph stage, during which they behave much as the dragonfly nymphs do. You can always recognize a damsel fly nymph by the three fins at the end of its tail. These fins are used as gills for breathing oxygen from the water and as rudders for steering the nymph when it moves through the water.

MAY FLIES. Another water insect with delicately veined wings is the May fly. You have probably seen them by the hundreds swarming around the lights on a summer evening near the water. They can easily be recognized by the two long, threadlike streamers that extend out from their tails.

The adult May fly lives for only a few hours, just long enough to fly in a swarm, find a mate, and lay eggs. Its mouth parts are useless, and it does not eat at all in its adult stage. If you have a chance to watch a swarm of May flies in their mating flight, notice how each insect soars straight upward, then drifts down again, then rises in a straight line, and back down once more, over and over again. Finally the female lays the eggs in the water, and the short life of the adults is over.

The nymphs that hatch from the eggs of May flies make up for the short lives of their parents. They spend several years in the nymph stage. During this time they feed on vegetable material — diatoms, desmids, algae, and other tiny water plants. Many of them, of course, never reach the adult stage because they are a favorite food for young fishes and for the larger preying, flesh-eating insects.

When the young adult May fly finally emerges from the water, it flies about for a short time. Then it sheds its skin, wings and all. It has a new skin with two new pairs of wings underneath. No other common insect, after it has once been able to fly, can shed its skin and have new wings underneath.

Dragonflies, damsel flies, and May flies have several features in common. They all have transparent, veined wings. They all pass through only three separate stages (egg, nymph, and adult), and all of them, in the nymph stage, are true water creatures, which do not need to come to the surface for oxygen.

CADDIS FLIES. Adult caddis flies look something like moths when they fly, but can be identified by their two long feelers,

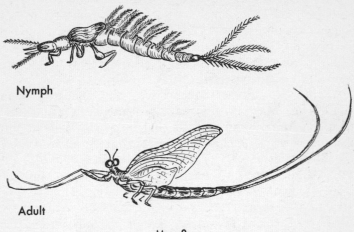

Nymph

Adult

May fly

which arch backward over their bodies. The adults are not particularly attractive or interesting. But the caddis fly larvae have a most unusual history. When each little wormlike larva hatches out of its egg, it builds itself a hard protective tube to live in. For building material it uses grains of sand, small pebbles, broken sticks, leaves, and old shells. It fastens the building material together with a waterproof silk it makes in its salivary glands. Each larva lives in its own tube. As the larva grows, it adds to its tube, which becomes longer and fatter as time goes on. When the larva moves about on the bottom of the pond or stream, it drags its tube behind it like a little trailer. The larvae eat both plant and animal material, and they are eaten by any larger creature that can catch them sticking out of their tubes.

When the time comes for the larva stage to end, each insect closes itself up in its own tube and enters the pupa stage. When it emerges from its tube-cocoon, it is an adult. It then rises to the surface of the water, dries its wings, and flies away in search of a mate. After mating in mid-air, the female lays hundreds of eggs on underwater plants and stones, or on plants that overhang the water, the eggs hatch into larvae, and the cycle continues, over and over again.

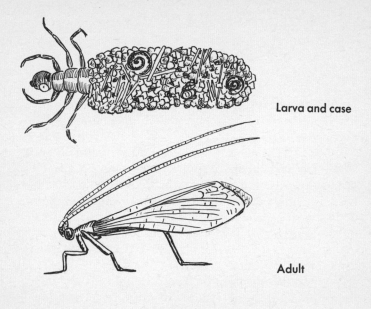

Larva and case

Adult

Caddis fly

ANURIDA. If you look for insects by the seashore, you may think that the beach is literally hopping with them. You will see sand fleas and sand hoppers burrowing in the sand at the water's edge or scampering in and out of the mazes of damp seaweed on the shore. These creatures are not insects, although they look and act very much like them. They are really sea animals of the same family as lobsters, shrimps, and crabs.

The truth is that there are very few insects living at the edge of the sea. This is a strange fact, considering that there are so very many insects in the world living in so many kinds of places. It would be interesting to discover why the seashore is not a good place for most insects to live.

There is one kind of true insect, however, that you may find at the edge of the ocean. It is called anurida. It is different from most other insects, not only because it lives by and on the sea, but also because it has no wings. It is blue-black and is usually found crawling over masses of seaweed, hiding under rocks, or skating on the surface film of a tide pool. It has a covering of thick hairs, which carry bubbles of air used by the insect when it goes under water. This unusual insect can carry enough air in this way to last it for several days.

On your hikes, picnics, and excursions around the water's edge, make a record of the different kinds of insects you see. Sit quietly and watch them as they hunt for prey, attack their live food, nibble on vegetable matter, move through the water, and perform other tasks, each according to its own peculiar nature. Human beings have to learn to secure food and shelter and safety and other things necessary to keep alive. But the little insects are born with all the knowledge and ability they need. A female caddis fly, for instance, will lay eggs on a leaf or twig that overhangs the water. When the larvae hatch out of the eggs they fall, plop-plop, into the water, which is the only place where they can live and breathe and catch their food during the larva stage. How does the mother caddis fly *know* that the eggs must be placed where the baby insects will drop directly into the water? No other insect has taught the caddis fly how or where to deposit the eggs. This is part of its natural insect knowledge. The things that insects and other creatures do because of some built-in knowledge, urge, or ability is called instinctive behavior. Instincts are what make them behave as they do. As you watch insect life about you, notice the things that insects do that are probably the result of instincts.

If you keep a notebook of your observations, with perhaps a few sketches from life, you can soon collect quite a bit of first-hand information about insect life. After you have had a chance to watch the ways in which a number of kinds of insects live in their natural world, you may want to have a closer look at one or two kinds. In the following chapter you will find some suggestions for catching specimens, taking care of them, and making observations and experiments.

FOUR

Experimenting with Water Insects

In order to make some scientific observations of water insects, you may want to capture some interesting specimens and bring them home with you. If you want only to get a closer look at a certain kind of water insect, all you will need is a small glass jar filled with some of the water in which the insect lives. Find one or two good specimens. Scoop them up with your kitchen strainer and dump them into the jar of water. Cover the jar with cheese cloth or a wire screen cover. Then you can look at the insects through your magnifying glass and make notes and sketches to help you remember what the insects are like. After a few hours of close observing, you can empty the jar carefully back into the lake or pond or stream and return your specimens to their natural home, where they can go on with their lives.

You may, however, want to keep your insects long enough to see how they eat, breathe, and grow. Some water insects will actually raise their families in homemade aquariums if you give them the things they need: oxygen to breathe, food to eat, and protection from their enemies. To provide these things, you will have to make the right kind of water home for each kind of insect you want to catch and raise. This is easy to do because all of the materials you need will be found in the same water where you find the insects. Following are some general suggestions to help you make a natural water home for the insects you catch.

For containers, use peanut-butter or mayonnaise jars, large pickle jars, glass or plastic refrigerator dishes, glass bowls, or any other kinds of glass or plastic containers. Make special little aquariums for small insects. If you keep large and small insects in the same jar, the large ones may eat up the smaller ones. It is also a good idea to keep each kind of meat-eating insect in a separate container. Plant eaters, of course, can be grouped together.

Begin each of your aquariums with a layer of sand or mud scooped from the bottom of the shallow part of the pond, lake, or stream. Dig up one or two tiny water plants and carefully put their roots into the soil at the bottom of your aquarium. Anchor the roots with pebbles or stones. Add water from the same source. You will have to carry home with you a jug or bottle of the same water so that you can refill your aquarium as the water evaporates. Regular city drinking water contains chemicals that are not good for water life. Also, drinking water does not contain any of the tiny, invisible plants or animals found in the waters of most ponds and streams. Such water life, which can be seen only through a microscope, serves as food for many kinds of water creatures. Since your aim is to create as natural a community as possible for your insects, you will want to use water, soil, stones, and plants from the insects' natural homes.

Some insects are more easily cared for than others. And some insects are more interesting in one stage than they are in other stages. Here are some suggestions about different kinds of insects to hunt for, and some hints about keeping them in aquariums.

The meat-eating insects are the ones that may eat each other up if different kinds or different sizes are put together. Since they depend upon other live creatures for food, you will have to feed some of them to others in order to keep the specimens alive. Often scientists keep one jar of very small specimens that are raised for the purpose of being used as food for the larger specimens. Every day or so, a few of the small creatures are added to each jar containing a larger insect. Large insects usually capture their food alive. But, when they are allowed to go hungry for two or three days, they can be trained to eat tiny pieces of raw meat. Put a very small bit of hamburger or raw liver on the end of a toothpick or broom straw. Twirl and move it around in the water near the insect.

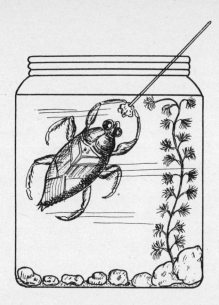

Water bug feeding

Chances are that the hungry insect will attack the meat.

Water insects are not dangerous, but the bite of one of the meat eaters can cause a nasty, painful swelling. Do not handle any of these creatures with your bare hands. Use a spoon, strainer, or pair of tweezers when you have to move them. Here are some insects to catch, raise, and experiment with.

WATER STRIDERS need shallow water in an aquarium jar with high walls. A large glass pickle jar is ideal. Put sand on the bottom, place a little water plant in the sand, and add a few striders, which you can scoop off the top of the water with a kitchen strainer. Cover the jar with cheesecloth or screen. The striders will eat the body juices of any smaller creatures that happen to drop into their paths or to bob up under their feet. They especially like small back swimmers. Let a strider go hungry for two days. Then drop a live ant in its path and watch the way it uses its beak and front legs to attack the ant. Try feeding a hungry water strider a bit of raw meat on a moving straw. If it will attack the meat, it can be raised easily in your aquarium. Use your hand lens to watch the way the surface film of water is pressed down by the strider's footsteps. Notice his hair-covered legs. Can you see that they are slightly oily?

BACK SWIMMERS also need a covered aquarium, for they, too, may try to fly away. They need some growing plants on which to lay eggs and also to hold onto when they go under water. They will eat practically any smaller water creatures — nymphs, larvae, tiny crustaceans, and other insects. They are especially quick to eat small water boatmen. With a drinking straw, push a back swimmer below the surface. Watch it bob right up again because of the air carried on its body hairs.

WATER BOATMEN will eat algae and larger water plants as well as tiny water creatures. Algae will grow naturally on and in your aquarium. Watch the boatmen scrape the algae off and eat it. Start a boatman aquarium in the early fall. The insects will lay eggs and raise young throughout the winter. Raise several generations of boatmen and use some of the tiny ones as food for other insects. Put a boatman and a back swimmer together. Notice how much they look alike and yet how they differ in two ways. The back swimmer travels on its back and the boatman swims right side up. The back swimmer uses its hind legs as oars and the boatman's oars are its large middle legs.

GIANT WATER BUGS need enough water plants in their aquarium to provide them a shadowy water home. They do not like sunlight. Keep their aquarium covered with a screen to keep them from flying away. They are fierce eaters and will attack practically any other small water creature. Let the water bug go hungry for a couple of days. Then offer it some raw meat on the tip of a toothpick. The bug will probably attack the meat with its powerful claws and beak. Try to find a male water bug with the eggs attached to its back. In about ten days from the time the eggs were laid, they will hatch into little wingless nymphs. Save the egg sack after it drops from the father's back. Examine it through your hand lens.

If you put some smaller water creatures (nymphs, tadpoles, tiny fish, diving beetles, etc.) into a jar in which you are keeping some giant water bugs, you can watch the way in which these vicious bugs attack, pierce, and eat the soft parts of their prey. Watch the process through your hand lens. This process is typical of the eating habits of all of the water bugs.

WATER SCORPIONS do well in a tall jar filled with water and a few growing plants. They prey on small underwater creatures. They may take raw meat from a moving straw if they are hungry enough. The most interesting feature of this insect is its snorkel, the long breathing tube that sticks out from its tail. Try this experiment. Put a small amount of water in the bottom of a milk bottle. Put a scorpion into the water. Then add more water, little by little. Watch how the insect will keep the end of its breathing tube above the top of the water.

WHIRLIGIG BEETLES may be caught in groups of five or six and kept in any glass container that has a wide mouth. They need some water plants on which to lay their eggs. The beetles and their small larvae eat small insects and other meat food.

DIVING BEETLES are interesting insects to catch and raise. You can find them hanging head down in the water, breathing through their tails. Their larvae are called *water tigers*. Some of them grow to be more than two inches long. They are fierce hunters. They have strong jaws and will attack live creatures that are even larger than themselves. Keep several diving beetles and their larvae in their own private aquarium. Feed them live insects or raw meat.

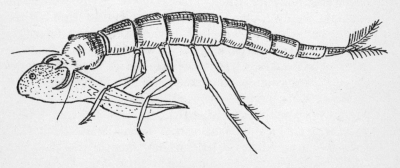

Water tiger

DRAGONFLY NYMPHS and DAMSEL FLY NYMPHS may be scooped up in the mud and sand on the bottom of a shallow pond or stream. Keep them in shallow water in a small jar with sand or soil and stones on the bottom and a growing plant that reaches up above the water level. They may be fed small insects and other tiny creatures. They may also take small bits of raw meat from the end of a broom straw. Dragonfly nymphs are a half to one-and-a-half inches long. Damsel fly nymphs are usually smaller and more delicate. You can recognize the nymphs of the damsel fly by the three flat, rudder-like gills on their tails.

Put one of the dragonfly nymphs in a shallow saucer or bowl filled with water. With a toothpick, open its mouth and uncoil its long under lip. Through your hand lens, examine the lip with its clawlike tip. Put the toothpick aside and drop a tiny live insect into the water in front of the nymph. If it is hungry, the nymph will shoot out its deadly lip, grasp the insect, and devour it. Next, put one drop of food color or ink on the water just back of the nymph's tail. Then touch the nymph's back suddenly with the toothpick. It will draw the colored water in and then expel it through its tail, thus shooting its body forward. Try this experiment several times with different nymphs in order to see how they jet-propel themselves by drawing water in and forcing it out of their tails.

If you feed your dragonfly and damsel fly nymphs, they may live in your aquarium through the winter or even longer. Then, one day, they will climb up the water plant into the air and fasten themselves to the plant as their skins split down the back. If you are lucky enough to be watching when this wonderful change takes place, you will see the water-living nymphs change before your eyes into adults, which will dry their damp, crumpled wings, spread them out in the sunshine, and then fly off as darting gossamer-winged creatures of the air. If you miss seeing the actual change, you will look at your aquarium one day and find that the nymphs are gone. But on the stems of the water plants, above the water level, you will find the split, empty skins from which the adults emerged.

CADDIS FLY LARVAE can be collected from underwater rocks and plants and from the mud and sand on the bottom of streams and ponds. You will find each larva in its own little tube or case. Keep the larvae in a shallow aquarium with sand, tiny pebbles and shells, and bits of bark and dead leaves on the bottom. Plant some tiny water plants in the sand. The caddis fly larvae will eat plant material, including the algae that will grow on and in the aquarium. Some kinds of caddis fly larvae will also eat bits of meat or small insects. You will have to experiment to discover what kinds of food your specimens will eat.

Examine the tubes through your hand lens and discover what materials have been used to make them. Look for grains of sand, broken shells, twigs, strands of plant materials, bits of bark, and tiny pebbles. As the larvae grow, they will make their cases larger, using the materials they find on the bottom of their aquarium home. If you put in some tiny colored beads, the larvae may add them to their tubes and you can see how the materials are joined together with the waterproof silk made by the insects. If you keep the larvae long enough, they will seal themselves into their tubes and become pupae, which will then change into adult winged insects. When an adult insect emerges from the pupa stage, it floats to the top of the water or climbs up the stem of a water plant and then flies off to live the rest of its life in the air.

If you have a large tank or bowl aquarium, you may want to make a mixed insect aquarium and watch nature take its course. You will want to keep the water fairly clear so that you can see what goes on in the aquarium. For this reason, try to use sand rather than mud for the bottom. In it plant some small water plants from the edge of the body of water where you will collect the insects. Use stones around the plants to hold the roots in place. Put a pan or saucer on the bottom of the aquarium. When you pour in the water, pour it onto the pan or saucer. This keeps the force of the water from digging a hole in the sand bottom. It also helps to keep the water clear. When you have filled the aquarium, remove the pan or saucer, adjust the plants, and press the stones firmly around their roots. Then let the aquarium stand for about a day until the water has become as clear as possible.

Meanwhile, you can begin to collect your insect specimens. Use your kitchen-strainer scoop to gather creatures from among the plants at the water's edge. After each dip, dump whatever you catch into a dishpan full of water. From there you can transfer them with a spoon to separate little jars and bottles. Dip deeper into the water for more specimens. Try to get samples of the different insects that live in the water where you are collecting. After you have dipped up as many as you want from the water plants, the surface of the water, and the water just below the surface, take your tin-can scoop and begin to scoop up samples of the bottom. As you dump each canful of bottom soil into the dishpan, look carefully for caddis fly tubes, insect eggs, the nymphs of dragonflies and damsel flies, and other creatures that live in and on the bottom mud and sand. You may find that you are collecting snails, tadpoles, tiny fish, and other water creatures as well as insects in different stages.

Put a few of each of the smallest creatures into your water-life aquarium. Do not put in any of the following: giant water bugs, large fish, turtles, or large tadpoles. Even one of these big eaters would eat up all the others in a very short time.

Keep your aquarium outdoors. Fit a piece of window screening over the top. Choose a location where it will get sun an hour or two a day and will be in the shade the rest of the time. With your hand lens, watch the water creatures carefully. Make notes on what you observe. Write a report, if possible with your own illustrations, of life and death in your experimental aquarium. You should be able to discover answers to questions like the following:

1. How many different kinds of insects were put into the aquarium? How many of each kind?

2. Which kinds of insects did you see capture and eat their prey?

3. Which kinds did you see being caught and eaten?

4. What kinds of animal life, other than insects, were put into the aquarium?

5. What happened to the noninsects? Which kinds were eaten? Which kinds ate other creatures?

And, of course, the most interesting part of the report will tell how the experiment turns out — which creatures, if any, survive the fierce eat-or-be-eaten competition of water life in your aquarium? Then, using your knowledge of the habits of different insects, try to figure out and explain why and how some creatures survived while others quickly disappeared. This experiment can show you, in a small way but right under your eyes, the life and death struggle that is going on all the time in the waters you explore.

FIVE

Life in Miniature

As you observed and experimented with water insects, you discovered that many of the small water creatures eat smaller water creatures, which eat still smaller creatures. And if you had eyes as powerful as a microscope, you could see that these tiny creatures feed on still tinier creatures. What, then, is the food of the very tiniest creatures that live in water? What is the very beginning of the food chain, in which each kind of water creature serves as food for something bigger than itself?

The very beginning of the food chain is the diatom, a water plant so small that there may be as many as a million of them in a single quart of water. They are so small that you cannot see what they look like without a microscope. And, there are so many of these tiny plants! They live and grow in lakes, ponds, rivers, and oceans. Scientists think that their total weight is probably greater than the weight of all the plants that grow on land!

While you cannot see separate diatoms, you can collect and see whole bunches of them. Try this experiment. Using your nylon water net (described in Chapter Two), sweep through the water of the ocean, or of a lake, pond, or stream. If you can, go out in a boat and trail the net through the water as the boat travels. Gradually the inside of the net will become coated with a film of slimy green and brown paste. The longer you trail the net in the water, the heavier the film of paste will become.

When you return to dry land, turn your net inside out and examine the paste. Feel it with your fingers. Smell it. Look at it through your hand lens. Some people say that it reminds them of thick pea soup. It usually smells more like some kind of fish or seaweed, however. Scrape off a bit of it and put it into a jar of clear water. Then look at the particles in the water through your hand lens. You may possibly be able to see tiny spots of green and spots of brown, but the separate plants that form the colors cannot be seen even with your magnifying glass. The brown and the green materials are two kinds of water plants called algae. The brown are the diatoms, the simplest and most important of all drifting plant life. The green plants are desmids, another of the simple algae.

If you could use a microscope to look at a few drops of the water in which you have placed the bits of green and brown ooze, you could discover what the separate little plants look like. Through a microscope you could see that the yellowish-brown diatoms have different shapes. Some are round, some oval, some boat-shaped, some curved, twisted, irregular. Each diatom is enclosed in a tiny glasslike box, which it manufactures. This box or glassy skeleton lasts long after the diatom itself is dead. When diatoms die, their skeletons drift silently down to the bottom, where they form deep layers of underwater flooring.

The one-celled diatom was one of the first plants to occur on the earth. And it still occurs today, still with the same simple structure it had billions of years ago. Without diatoms, there would be little if any animal life in the seas and fresh waters of the earth. If there were no diatoms, there would be none of the larger water creatures — and man would lack an important source of food. So the microscopic diatom, which is essential to all water life, is also important to us!

If you could look at the green algae through a microscope, you would discover some more unusual shapes. The desmids are round, crescent-shaped, straight-sided, or curved. Each one seems to be divided by a clear band in the middle. Other green algae you might see are chains of separate cells connected to form a long, twisting rope. You may sometimes notice green slimy threads drifting on the surface of a pond. These threads are algae, like the tiny green plants in the film of green and brown paste in your nylon net.

The smallest and simplest of the water animals are the pro-

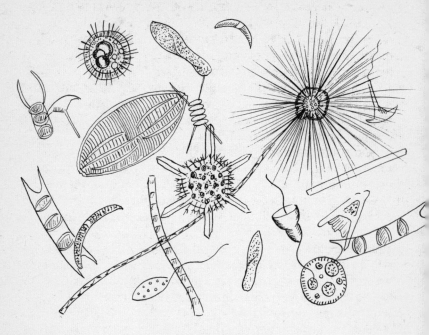

Microscopic plants and animals

tozoa. Like the diatoms, protozoa are far too small to be seen except through a microscope. These and other tiny water animals and plants drift with the currents of the sea and other bodies of water. The plants are not fastened down. The animals have no ways of moving about on their own. Because they are free-floating organisms, these tiny bits of water life are called *plankton*, a Greek word that means "wanderers." Animal plankton feed on plant plankton. Plant plankton are fed by certain chemicals made from the dead animal plankton. Animal and plant plankton, then, live on one another, and together they provide food for the tiny shelled animals of the sea. These animals, called crustaceans, are the main food of herring, the most abundant fish in the sea. The herring in turn are eaten by larger fish, the cod, haddock, and tuna. And man is one of the animals to eat the tuna and other large fish. It is interesting to picture this food chain and to realize that microscopic plant plankton provide the basic food for all the living, moving creatures of all the waters of the earth. It is quite a job for plants that are too small to be seen even with a good magnifying glass!

It is not possible to do much experimenting with microscopic plants and animals unless you have a good microscope and other scientific equipment. You can, however, collect and get a good look at some of the tiny animals that are just big enough to be seen with a magnifying glass, and others that you can just barely see with the unaided eye. To do this, make a miniature aquarium.

For your aquarium, use a peanut-butter or mayonnaise jar, half-pint size. Go to the edge of some small inland body of water — a quiet pond in a park, a pool in the woods, an irrigation ditch in which the water is not flowing swiftly, or a lake with a mud bottom. Use your tin-can scoop, a trowel, a small shovel, or a large spoon. Scoop up some of the underwater mud from a spot near the edge of the water. Put one large spoonful of the mud on the bottom of your jar. Add a few small sticks and bits of dead plant material you may be able to pick up under the water. If there is any floating plant material on the water, add a few bits of this, too. Then fill the jar with water from the same source. Set the jar aside for several hours to allow the water to clear. By the end of that time, the tiny water creatures you have captured will have made themselves at home and you can look for them through your magnifying glass.

There will, of course, be hundreds of plants and animals in your jar too small to be seen except through a microscope. But you will be amazed at how many others you can see through your hand lens, and even some large enough to be seen with the unaided eye. Here are some things to look for — living things that are typical of the miniature life found in most fresh-water ponds and streams.

First of all, you may have captured some of the relatively large creatures that you have already observed in your work with insects — nymphs, larvae, caddis fly tubes. Also, you may find some little snails, a tiny fish or two, and perhaps a little crayfish. If so, it is a good idea to take these "big" animals out of your miniature aquarium. Although you will be doing some experiments with these fellows later on, right now you are after the very, very small things that live in ponds and streams.

Among the miniatures, you may have captured some interesting fresh-water worms, very small, but possibly large enough to be noticed without your magnifying glass. You can read about these tiny fresh-water worms in Chapter Ten.

HYDRAS are probably the most unusual of the water creatures you are likely to find in your little aquarium. After the mud has settled and the water has cleared, look for tiny thread-like bits clinging to plant material, to the sides of the jar, or just hanging from the film on the top of the water. Though the hydras are usually large enough to be seen with the naked eye, they are very small animals, only one-tenth to one-half an inch long. Each one looks like a short thread fringed at one end. The fringe is a group of waving arms, called tentacles. The tentacles make the hydra look something like an octopus. And, indeed, the hydra uses its waving arms in much the way an octopus uses its tentacles for catching food. Each of the hydra's tentacles can be used independently. A tentacle reaches out, encircles a water flea or other small water creature, stings it senseless with the stinging cells that run along each tentacle, and then, with the help of several tentacles, stuffs the captured animal into its mouth.

There are usually six tentacles, but there may be as many as ten. The hydra was named for Hydra, the nine-headed dragon that was killed by Hercules, according to Greek mythology. The little hydra may have nine waving arms, but never nine heads. In fact, it doesn't really have any head at all, though it has one large mouth, an opening in the middle of the circle of tentacles. The mouth is the only opening to the body, which is an elastic tube with the ring of tentacles at one end and a kind of foot at the other.

The hydra's foot, or base, can serve as an anchor when the hydra is at rest and can help it along when the hydra moves.

The foot can also secrete a sticky fluid and can make a gas bubble, enclosed in a film of mucus. When this happens, the bubble raises the hydra to the surface, where the bubble bursts. Then the mucus spreads out like a raft and the hydra hangs, tentacles down, from the underside.

Since the hydra's body can stretch or contract, and the tentacles, too, can become several times the body length, a hydra is sometimes several times as long as it is at other times. When it is disturbed, a hydra can make itself very small indeed. It draws in its tentacles, contracts its body, and shrinks into a tiny green or brown ball. But when relaxed and at home,

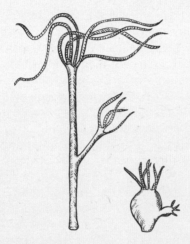

Budding hydra, stretched out and contracted

the hydras will interest you for hours with their antics. They will attach themselves by their bases to the glass walls of the jar while their tentacles will wave freely about in search of food. Or they will inch along on the glass, in a sort of hand-over-hand motion, using their tentacles to pull themselves along. Or they will move through the water, doing cartwheels as they go, swinging their arms and stretching their bases out in search of a fresh place to anchor. Watch your hydras through your magnifying glass and notice the different ways in which they move.

Hydras reproduce in two ways. In the fall they lay eggs, which hatch in spring. They also create new hydras by sprouting buds. Each bud can grow into a complete adult. As it grows, the new hydra stays attached to the parent hydra for a long time.

Hydras are important to know about because they are examples of an interesting animal family that includes jellyfish, corals, sea anemones, and other unusual water creatures. These animals have two features in common: each one has a body with a hollow place in it that serves as a stomach and complete digestive tract; and each one has some sort of tentacles with stinging cells.

WATER FLEAS are some of the very, very tiny water life likely to be in your aquarium. They are so small that you can barely see them with the unaided eye. But they are big enough to be seen easily through your magnifying glass. You will see them moving up and down in the water, very fast. They look like tiny hopping fleas, though they are not really fleas at all. Water fleas feed on the microscopic plants and animals found in all natural bodies of water. They, in turn, are eaten by hydras, and by insects, tadpoles, and other water creatures.

Water fleas are tiny crustaceans. Crustaceans are animals that have hard shells, or crusts, over soft bodies. As crustaceans, water fleas are related to crayfish, lobsters, crabs, and shrimps. The scientific name for a water flea is daphnia.

A daphnia is usually transparent. Its tiny body is enclosed in a bivalve shell, that is, a two-part shell. Through the shell can be seen a regularly beating heart. In front of the heart is a single eye. Back of the heart is a pouch filled with eggs. A daphnia will lay eggs with thin shells in the summer and thick-shelled eggs in the winter.

Other tiny crustaceans to look for in your miniature aquarium are the cyclops and fairy shrimp.

CYCLOPS gets its name from the one-eyed giant, Cyclops, of Greek mythology. It is certainly not a giant, but it does have a single eye, a red one, in its tiny greenish body. This little crustacean often has a sac full of eggs on each side of its tail. There is one kind of cyclops that lives in the sea, where it exists in

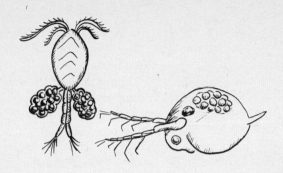

Cyclops and daphnia

such great numbers that it is the main food of a certain kind of whale.

FAIRY SHRIMPS live in fresh-water pools, where they are very common. They are pinkish in color, and nearly transparent. They swim on their backs. They lay their eggs in the summer. The eggs become buried in the mud, where they are protected through the winter. The following spring the eggs hatch out. Some fairy shrimps grow to be an inch long.

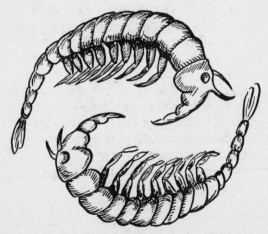

Fairy shrimps

If you do not find many specimens of miniature water creatures in your first peanut-butter-jar aquarium, try the experiment over and over again. Keep a record of the animals you do find. Watch them through your magnifying glass. Make sketches of the way you see them. Keep a record of them in a notebook. Whenever you go to a different body of fresh water, start a new miniature aquarium, sampling the bottom mud from as many ponds, streams, ditches, and lakes as you can explore.

You can also make a miniature aquarium by getting jars of water from an old aquarium tank or pool at a pet store. Any aquarium water in which water plants have been allowed to grow, and in which there are no fish or larger water life, is likely to have a rich collection of miniature life. Sometimes a fish store will have tanks of water plants outside, or neglected algae-filled tanks in a back room. If you bring your own jars, you can usually get them filled for the asking. Explain to the dealer that you are looking for daphnia, hydras, water worms, and other tiny water animals. Keep your jar of aquarium water in a sunny window. It will grow its own green algae, and the water fleas will multiply rapidly.

In a few days you are likely to have a crowded jar of hopping and darting water creatures. You can divide your collection by pouring some off into new jars. If you have several hydras, you will want to keep them in a separate jar and feed them some of the water fleas each day. If you keep your hydras in the same jar with the daphnia and cyclops, you will soon have only hydras.

With a good magnifying glass in your hand, you can explore the lives of hundreds of tiny, busy water animals. Little by little, you will become familiar with the tiny creatures described here, and probably, if you keep exploring, you will discover other water creatures, which you will want to look up in science books that tell about all the fresh-water animals that are found in this country.

SIX

Shells and Shell Collecting

If you go to the seashore, you have surely held sea shells in your hands. Perhaps you have a shell collection. Many people do, because shells are beautiful to look at and interesting to own. As you walk along the beach, you will find different kinds of shells, many of them cleaned, bleached, and polished smooth by the actions of sea and sand and sun. You may think of shells as lovely pink, white, yellow, or pearly-colored things, like some of the ones you have at home or have seen in collections — rainbow-colored abalone shells, delicate, fluted scallop shells, rosy-pink baby clam shells, silvery pearl moon shells, or the giant conch with its pink and gold lining. There are jingle shells as delicate-looking as a baby's fingernail; limpets like little volcanoes or like tiny coolie hats; there are shells shaped like tops, turbans, pears, wings, saucers, razors, pens, tusks, olive pits, slippers, boats, helmets, figs, coffee beans, drills, tulips, and bubbles. There are shells tinted yellow, green, silvery white, gold, brown, purple, gray, tan, pink, and almost black. There are shells decorated with fanlike ribs, circles, knobs, bumps, whorls, spirals, dots, scallops, stripes, and many combinations of these. Interesting, beautiful sea shells! No wonder so many people collect and keep them.

The lovely shell you pick up on the beach is likely to be a dead shell. It is the outside covering of an interesting boneless animal. When the animal was alive, its shell probably looked quite different from the bleached and polished thing you find in the sand. In order to enjoy collecting shells, you will want to discover for yourself something about the interesting creatures that make them, the mollusks.

Some mollusks can be found on land, more of them in fresh

water, and most of them in the salt waters of the sea. About 90,000 different kinds of mollusks are known to scientists. Some of these are known to everybody because we use their soft bodies as food. Oysters, clams, and scallops are common foods all over the United States. Abalone is eaten in the states that border the Pacific Ocean. And mussels, snails, whelks, periwinkles, and some of the other mollusks are prized as food in other parts of the world.

Wherever you live, there are probably some kinds of shell makers in the waters nearby. In fact, even in areas far from water, interesting shells can be found. In layers of rock on some deserts and in some mountains, shells mark places where prehistoric bodies of water once made homes for the ancient mollusks.

There are many kinds of mollusks, but most of them have several features in common. One of these is a flat, muscular foot. A snail uses its foot for crawling over surfaces. A clam uses its foot for plowing and digging through sand and mud.

Another common mollusk feature is a mantle, the part of the animal's body that makes the shell. The mantle has many tiny tubes that secrete bits of calcium mineral, which the mantle has taken from the water. The calcium mineral is mixed with a material like horn, which makes the shell strong. Shells are built rapidly. When a shell gets a hole or crack in it, the mantle repairs it in a few days. You can find shells with scars, showing where repairs have been made. Among the tiny tubes in the mantle are some that produce a kind of dye. Sometimes the dye tubes are arranged in a regular order. The shell made by such a mantle will have a regular color pattern. But there are many mollusks with color tubes that can be controlled by the animal itself. In such cases, each shell has an individual pattern.

Most shells are made in three layers. The outside is thin and horny. It is a coating that protects the other layers from the acid that is dissolved in water. The middle layer is usually fairly thick. The inner layer, the part next to the animal's soft body, is a lining of mother-of-pearl. This is smooth and shiny

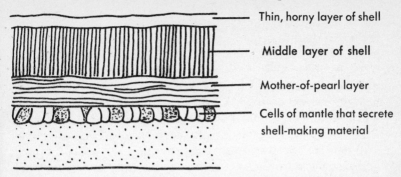

Thin, horny layer of shell

Middle layer of shell

Mother-of-pearl layer

Cells of mantle that secrete
shell-making material

Cross section of the shell and mantle of a clam

and sometimes glows with many colors as light falls on the thin layers of shell material.

Some mollusks eat only plant material. Some eat only meat. And there are some that will eat both. Many mollusks have jaws, and many have a special organ called a radula, which is like a tongue with rows of sharp points. As the animal draws food into its mouth, the radula tears and shreds the food to bits. In some cases the radulas are as strong as drills or files and can work their way through the shell of another mollusk.

One of the most interesting things you can do when you discover living mollusks is to watch them through your magnifying glass while they are feeding. Each kind of shell maker has its own special ways of getting its food — sucking it up, tearing it apart, surrounding it with its own flesh, straining it out of the sea water, or just gulping it down whole. As you get acquainted with mollusks, see how many different ways of eating you can discover and observe.

Like all other animals, mollusks need oxygen. Some of them breathe through places in their mantles, which act as lungs. Such mollusks can breathe air. Most fresh water snails and all land snails breathe in this way. Other mollusks breathe as fish do, through gills, which take oxygen from the water.

Most mollusks lay eggs. Some kinds of mollusks have separate males and females. With other kinds, both sexes are in one individual. Certain mollusks lay only a few eggs a season — fifteen, twenty, forty, or a hundred. But others lay thousands or even millions of eggs a year. A single oyster, for instance, produces five hundred *million* eggs in one season! The eggs and young of the oyster meet with so many dangers in the ocean that millions of extra eggs are needed just to keep the oyster families going. Some of the other kinds of mollusks have few dangers and so fewer eggs are needed.

There are two main ways of collecting shells. The most common way is to pick up the dead shells that are washed up on the beach or are found in shallow water. Such shells are usually clean, all of the flesh having been eaten out by sea animals. The shells themselves have been washed, scoured, and bleached. It is easy to collect large quantities of shells by the simple beachcombing method.

If you want to have an accurate, scientific collection, however, beachcombing is not the best way to collect shells. The very elements that have so thoroughly cleaned and polished the shells have also broken and discolored most of them. Rarely can you find a fresh and perfect shell washed ashore. For perfect shells you will have to collect the shell makers alive and then prepare and clean the shells carefully.

To catch mollusks alive, wade into the *shallow* water and explore tide pools, rocks, the areas under wharfs and docks, wooden and concrete pilings, sand bars, mud flats, and the lowest area of the beach, where it is washed by waves. Wear shorts or your swim suit, and protect your feet from sharp rocks and broken shells by wearing tennis shoes. For collecting in Florida, in other tropical areas, or among coral reefs, protect your legs from sharp coral by wearing long pants tied around your ankles. Also, take a partner with you. *Never* go out into deep water after shells. You will find more than you need on the rocks near shore, in the shallow tide pools, and in the mud or sand at the water's edge. Listed below are some handy things to have with you when you go exploring for live mollusks:

A cloth or netting bag in which to carry the specimens you catch

Plastic jars or bottles for the rare or delicate specimens

A rake or hoe, the kind used by clam diggers, for digging
out the mollusks that bury themselves in sand or mud

A tire iron, short crowbar, chisel, or strong putty knife
for moving rocks and for prying some specimens from
their perches

Do your collecting on familiar ground, where there are
people around and where you *know* that the water is shallow
and without any sudden holes or drop-offs. And, if possible,
have a companion or fellow collector with you. Two collectors
working together are usually more than twice as efficient as
one working alone.

When you get your shell creatures home, most of them will
be dead. If you are not able to clean them at once, put them
into a pan or bucket and cover them with water. Then, after
you have rested up from your shell hunt (perhaps the following day), you can empty and clean your specimens.

The best way to prepare the tiny shells, especially the
twisted shells of little sea snails, is to treat them with a chemical that shrinks up the flesh without harming the delicate
shells. This chemical is *formaldehyde*, which an adult can buy
at the drugstore. Formaldehyde is usually sold as a 40 per cent
solution. Use one part of the solution and ten parts of water.
This makes a 4 per cent solution, which is strong enough for
your purpose. Drop the little mollusks into this solution and
let them soak for several days. Then take them out, wash them
in fresh water, and let them dry. By this time most or all of
the flesh will be gone and your shells will be clean and in good
condition.

Large mollusks can be cleaned in the following way. Put
them into a large pan. Cover them with fresh water. Place on
the stove and heat slowly until the water begins to boil. Then
move the pan from the stove to a place where it can cool off.
When the shells are cool, take them one by one and carefully
scrape out all of the flesh, or as much of it as possible without
scratching the shell. Flat shells of clams and similar animals
are easy to clean. The shells open up and the insides can be
slipped out or scraped away. But for many of the spiral,
twisted snail shells you will need to use a strong wire, a knit-

ting needle, or a crochet hook to unscrew the animal's body from its shell.

As you remove the fleshy bodies of mollusks from their shells, you will have a good chance to discover some of their interesting parts. In cleaning bivalves, look for the muscles that open and close the shell. These tough pieces of flesh usually hold on to the shell even after the rest of the flesh has been cooked away. If so, scrape them off gently and then look at the spots on the inside of the shell where the muscles were attached. Notice, too, the long siphon tubes dangling from many of the bivalves. Look at the inside parts too. Mollusks have heart, liver, stomach, intestines, and other internal organs. You may be able to locate some of them. As you begin to clean out the univalve mollusks, you are sure to find the operculums, the little covers of hornlike material with which the animals can seal themselves inside their shells. You will read more about bivalves and univalves in the next two chapters.

When you have done all you can to clean a shell and find that there is still some flesh sticking to it, you can get it absolutely clean by placing it on an anthill. The ants will soon eat off the bits of meat and leave the inside of the shell polished clean.

Often the outside surface of a shell is covered with algae, worm tubes, barnacles, and other tiny sea life, forming an unattractive crust. This can best be removed by scraping with a strong, blunt knife, or using a metal nail file, or sanding with fine, strong sandpaper. Then scrub with a stiff brush. After the scraping and scrubbing, wash the shell in clear water and then soak it in a solution of Clorox, Purex, or other bleaching liquid. Use one part bleach to eight parts of water. Let the shell soak for several hours, taking it out and examining it every half hour or so. The idea is to soak the shells long enough to remove the dirt and growths, but not long enough to destroy the shell's own outer layer. Sometimes, however, the natural outer skin of a shell may be so ugly that you will want to remove it and thus expose the more attractive inner layer. In such a case, allow the shell to soak in the bleach solution until the shell's thin outer layer can be scrubbed away. This may take several days.

After your shells have been cleaned, washed, and dried, they may look dull and colorless. If so, take a piece of soft cloth, moisten it in a bit of salad oil (peanut, soybean, or corn oil) or in some clear machine oil, and rub each shell, inside and out. The oil will bring out the natural color and shine of the shells. It will also help to preserve them. If, after a time, your shells lose their color and shine, wipe them again with oil. Some collectors make the mistake of coating their shells with shellac or clear lacquer, which gives them a hard and unnatural coating and spoils their soft, glowing beauty. Oil, on the other hand, will soak into the shell and restore its color, which was originally made by a kind of oil. As the oil dries out, the shell loses some of its color. When you rub on more oil, the color comes back.

Whether your collection is made up of dead shells you have gathered on the beach, or of specimens you have caught alive and prepared yourself, or some of each, you will need things in which to keep them. Strong egg cartons, with their twelve little compartments, are ideal for keeping your collection in order while you work on it. Delicate shells can be placed in nests of cotton or Kleenex. Tougher shells can simply be piled into the compartments. A separate carton can be used for each kind of shell. You can also exhibit your shells in egg cartons, which can be painted deep blue or black in order to make the shells stand out. The inside of the cover can be used for labels or information about the shells.

Another easy and effective way of making a permanent shell collection is to cement the shells to the bottom of a shallow cardboard box. The kind of box in which ladies' hosiery is sold is just right for small- and medium-sized shells. For larger shells, you will need deeper boxes. If you are making a large collection, use a separate box for each kind of shell. Arrange the shells in rows, from the smallest specimen you have to the largest that will fit into the box. Or arrange the shells in different positions so that all sides can be seen. Use transparent airplane model cement to fasten the shells to the cardboard bottom of the box. Leave the box flat while the cement is drying. After about twelve hours, the shells will be stuck tight. On the inside of the cover of the box, paste a sheet of paper on which you have written or typed something interesting about the kind of mollusk that makes shells like those in the box. Finally, you may want to paint the outside of the box or to cover it with paper on which you have drawn or painted a sea picture. Your own collection of such traylike boxes of shells could grow to be something valuable as well as interesting.

Some people like to specialize in their shell collecting. As you read more about some of the different kinds of shells, and especially as you explore your own neighborhood and find out what kinds of shells you are likely to find, you may decide to collect only certain kinds. A very interesting, beautiful, and delicate collection is one in which all specimens are shells under an inch in size. Some are so tiny that they must be viewed through a magnifying glass, which reveals the dainty perfection of each miniature shell. Little matchboxes, with their sliding drawers, have been used to house such collections. The boxes have been painted sea blue on the inside. Then the tiny shells have been glued to the bottom of the box, in straight rows, according to size. A label, telling the kind of shell and the place found, is pasted to the top of each box.

Large, small, or of different sizes, shells are fun to find, collect, prepare, and exhibit. They cost no money, are beautiful to look at, and they will last — if not *forever* — at least for a long, long time.

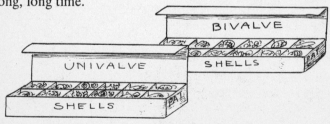

Shell collection in egg cartons

SEVEN

Univalve Mollusks

As soon as you begin to collect shells, you will want to know something about the different kinds you find and about the animals that make them. Then, little by little, you will get to know the main groups of shell makers and the names and habits of the most common kinds.

When you look at a snail, a clam, or an oyster, you may think that the shape of its body depends upon its shell. But it is really the other way around. The body, and especially the mantle, determines the form that its shell will take. If the mantle is all in one piece, the animal will have a single shell. If the mantle is in two parts (two lobes) the animal will have two shells, which are fastened together at the back with a strong hinge. One of the first steps in organizing your shell collection is to separate the univalves from the bivalves.

Univalves are also known as gastropods, which means "belly-footed." A gastropod does not have its belly in its foot, but it does have its one big foot in its middle, which in most animals is the belly region. Gastropods are mainly snails and snail-like mollusks. Each has a head with eyes, tentacles, mouth, and radula, and a single flat foot for creeping or for holding itself to a solid base. Land snails (the kinds you find in gardens and woodlands), fresh-water snails, and sea snails are all gastropods. So are giant conches, tiny periwinkles, flat abalones, and cone-shaped limpets. There are some gastropods that have no shells at all (slugs) and some that have very small shells hidden in their fleshy bodies (sea hares).

Some gastropods are vegetarians. Others eat meat. Most of them have mouths with jaws that draw in the food as the file-like radula tears it up. Most snails have spiral shells covering

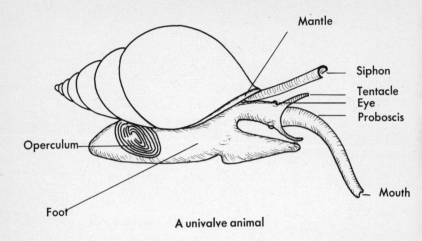

A univalve animal

twisted bodies. Some shells coil to the right and others to the left. An interesting part of a gastropod is its operculum. This is a horny cover that can close the opening when the animal withdraws into its shell. Sometimes the operculum fits so tightly that the animal can seal itself into its shell home, where it can hold in enough water to keep alive even when out of the water for a long time.

There are hundreds and hundreds of kinds of gastropods. Here are some of the most common kinds found on both the Atlantic and the Pacific coasts.

PERIWINKLES are small (one-half to one inch) shells, spotted or mottled, and usually a dull brownish color. They are fat and rounded at the open end. They feed on seaweed and other algae. Periwinkles are very common on most beaches here and in Europe. We do not eat periwinkles in the United States, but there are many countries where they are used as food.

Capture some living periwinkles and try the following experiments. First, drop a couple of them into a jar filled with sea water. Add a few pieces of seaweed. If the periwinkles are undisturbed for a while, they will begin to feed. Watch them through your magnifying glass. Drop two or three periwinkles into a glass of fresh drinking water. Notice how the animals withdraw into their shells and close the shell openings with their operculums. Leave two or three other periwinkles out of water entirely. Notice that they, too, seal themselves in by means of tight-fitting operculums. With the help of these wonderful little covers, the periwinkles are able to keep the moisture of the sea inside their shells and to keep out the fresh water. In this way, periwinkles can keep alive for many days away from the sea. After you have kept your specimens out of sea water for four or five days, put them back into a tide pool or into a little pool you can make in the sand and allow the waves to fill. Watch what happens as each periwinkle is returned to salt water. It will gradually open its operculum, withdraw from its shell, and begin searching for something to eat.

To discover how periwinkles move about, mark some of them and keep track of them over a period of time. Do it in this way. Find some periwinkles in a tide pool. Take them out one at a time. Dry off the shell and mark it with a dot of dark red nail polish. Let the polish dry. Then return each periwinkle to the place where you found it. As you look for your marked specimens each day, you will notice how many of them stay in the same area, how many disappear, and how many die and leave behind them their marked shells. You can, of course, study the movement of any kind of shell-bearing animal by marking the shell with some kind of waterproof enamel and then keeping a record of how and where you find it each day.

Periwinkle shell

TOP SHELLS are from one-half inch to four inches high. They are shaped like spinning tops. Some have a very heavy operculum, which fits exactly into the shell opening.

HORN SHELLS are commonly found on mud flats, among seaweed, and in shallow tide pools. They are only one-fourth to one-and-one-half inches long, but attractive, slim shells, with ten to fifteen spirals.

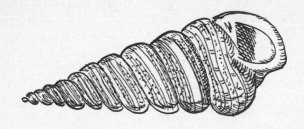

Horn shell

MOON SHELLS are fat and round and smooth and colored silvery white or pinkish tan. They are lovely shells to find, but the living animal is a great menace to other mollusks. These little shells (usually only an inch or two across) enclose a preying animal that has an enormous foot and an enormous appetite for the flesh of other animals. It attacks its prey and smothers it with its large, fleshy foot. When frightened, the moon snail draws its whole body, huge, fat foot and all, into its round shell and closes the shell with its horny operculum. But, since it is very crowded inside the shell, the snail cannot stay in there very long.

A moon snail lays its eggs in a jelly-like sheet, which it cements together with sand and forms into a collar shape around its foot. When the eggs hatch, the sand collar crumbles, releasing thousands of moon-snail larvae. They are washed by waves and tide into the sea, where they grow into adults.

MUREX, like the moon snails, are flesh eaters, feeding mainly on bivalves. Their shells, from an inch to six inches high, have heavy ridges in them and are often covered with

Moon snail with sand collar

sharp points or spines. The murex usually live in deep water, but their empty shells are often washed to shore.

WHELKS are both small and large univalves. The big ones are the giants of the gastropods. Sometimes they get to be more than a foot long. They are meat-eating animals, preying upon bivalves, which they pierce with their powerful drill-like tongues. Whelks are also scavengers, cleaning up dead animal material. You may find whelk shells along the beach at any time. In summer, though, you may find something even more interesting — strings of whelk egg cases. The cases seem to be made of a kind of parchment paper. They are fastened together in a string several feet long. Each case is filled with eggs or, if the eggs have already hatched, with tiny whelk shells, which will leave the egg cases and be carried by the waves to shallow water. There they can find tiny sea life to feed on. Most whelks, whatever their size, have a long tube-like end on one side of the shell. This projection of shell holds and protects the long siphon through which the living animal takes in the water from which its gills remove oxygen. There are many kinds of whelks in American and British waters. You could, if you wished, specialize in this one kind of shell. Specimens of the whelk shells, their different kinds of egg cases, and their life histories could keep your interest for a long time.

CONCHES and HELMETS are animals found only in tropical waters. They include some of the largest and most predatory

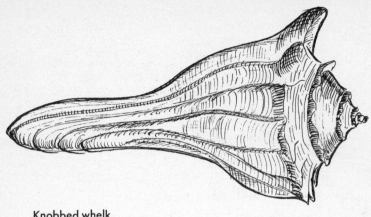

Knobbed whelk

univalves. They eat bivalves, other univalves, and dead fish. Shells of the queen conch are commonly used for doorstops. The helmet shells are used for making cameos. To make a cameo, an artist carves a head in the white outer layer of the shell and then carves away all white in the background. This leaves a delicate white figure against a tan, brown, or deep pink background.

LIMPETS are small animals, usually an inch or so long. In their baby stage, limpets grow spiral shells. But as they get larger, they form flat shells, slightly cone-shaped. Like all snails, the limpet has a single foot. With its foot the limpet can attach itself so tightly to a rocky surface that you will have to use a strong knife and a great deal of force to pry it loose. In

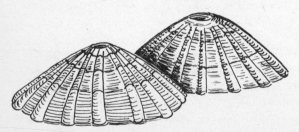

Limpet shells

some wonderful way, the limpet manages to grind away enough of the rock surface with its shell to make a perfect fit between the rock and the edge of its shell. When a rock is too hard to be ground down by the shell, the edge of the shell is worn away to fit the rock. Thus, each limpet has its own water-tight rocky perch. When it moves, which it does only when covered by the tide, it moves only a few feet and somehow is able to return again to its own personally fitted place.

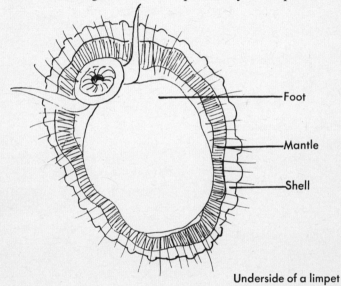

Foot

Mantle

Shell

Underside of a limpet

BOAT SHELLS or SLIPPER SHELLS are small snails that live much as limpets do. Their attractive little shells have a shelf across one end. They are only one-fourth to two inches long, and are often washed up on the beach.

ABALONES are interesting mollusks that live in fairly warm waters, especially in the Pacific. They are commonly found along the coast of California. Some kinds grow to be seven inches or more across. The live animal lives much as the limpet does. Its powerful muscle foot holds tightly to a rock, and its strong, saucer-shaped shell fits down over its body. It fastens itself so securely that a heavy metal tool must be used to pry it loose. Abalones are protected by strict conservation laws. Only people who know the legal size and season for abalone fishing may take them. If you see a live abalone clinging to a rock near the shore, do not disturb it. Just look at it carefully and notice how its dark, rough outer shell makes it look like a part of the rock. The shell has a row of holes in it. These holes let the water in and out, and with the water comes the food and oxygen the animal needs. As the shell grows, new, larger holes are formed and the older, smaller holes are closed up. But you can still see the marks where the little holes used to be. If you have a chance to examine an empty abalone shell, you will notice at once the lovely, iridescent mother-of-pearl on the inside of the shell. This is sometimes used for making jewelry. If you examine the shell, you will see that, like a true gastropod, the abalone has a spiral shell. The main part of the shell, however, is a single large whorl, which gets bigger and bigger as the animal grows. Sometimes small abalone shells are washed up on the beaches of Southern California. If you find one, it will be a precious addition to your collection.

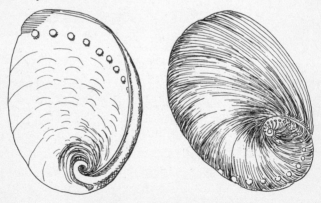

Abalone shell

There are, of course, many, many more kinds of gastropods that live in the sea. There are also many varieties of the gastropods described above. Part of the fun of exploring the seashore is to discover new kinds of shells for your collection.

Even if you do not live near the ocean, you can find some kinds of univalves to collect. Here are some of the more common fresh-water gastropods.

POND SNAILS are found all over the world in ponds, lakes, and ditches. One kind breathes air, for which it must keep coming to the surface. It lays eggs. Its shell is long, with long, thin spirals. It is tan or brown. Another kind of pond snail breathes oxygen from the water and bears its young alive. This kind lives on the muddy bottoms of lakes and ponds. Its shell is somewhat fat and round. It is colored brown, olive green, or purple and may be decorated with dark bands or ridges.

There are many other kinds of fresh-water snails. POUCH, RAM'S-HORN, WHEEL, and GREEN are some whose names describe them. There are also small fresh-water LIMPETS, which live and behave much as their salt-water cousins do.

EIGHT

Bivalves and Other Mollusks

As you explore the seashore, you will find bivalves as well as univalves. About four-fifths of all the bivalve mollusks in the world live in the sea. Often when you pick up a common shell on the beach, you pick up only *half* of the shell that the animal wore when alive. The two halves, which may look very much alike, were originally fastened together by a muscle hinge. After the animal died, its soft body was eaten by other sea creatures. The fleshy hinge decayed, and the shell was washed ashore in two pieces. Once in a while you may be lucky enough to find a complete bivalve shell, with its two halves still joined together by the hinge. Of course, if you can collect some of your specimens alive, you may be able to remove the flesh (as described in Chapter Six) without destroying the hinge.

Bivalves are well-developed animals, with gills for breathing and a wedge-shaped foot used for digging into sand and mud. They have no heads, eyes, radulas, or tentacles. Most of them have two tubes, called siphons, which can be pushed out when the animal opens its shell. Water goes in through one tube, giving the animal both oxygen and food. Then the water is expelled through the other tube, carrying away the waste material. In order to live, bivalves must have a continuous supply of clean, food- and oxygen-carrying water.

It is often possible to tell how old a bivalve mollusk is — or how old it was when it died — by counting the rings on its shell. Like tree rings, growth rings on shells mark the periods of rapid growth that occur once a year. Some shells have rings grouped together in bands, each band of rings marking a year's

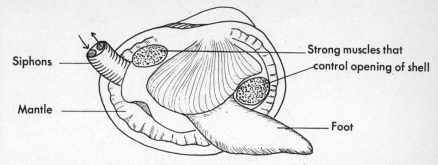

Siphons

Mantle

Strong muscles that control opening of shell

Foot

Inside of a bivalve animal

growth. Examine some bivalve shells and try to figure out how long it took the mollusks to build them.

Often you will find a bivalve shell with a neat round hole in it. This tells a story of tragedy. The hole was drilled by one of the flesh-eating univalves — a moon snail, whelk, oyster drill, or other carnivorous snail. The helpless bivalve, with its hard shell drilled into by a preying univalve, was then slowly eaten alive. Many bivalves lose their lives in this way. Many others are gathered and used as food for man. Bivalves have been a favorite food since prehistoric times. As you read about the most common bivalve mollusks, notice how many of them you have long been familiar with — in sea-food salads, on the half-shell, deep fried, and in stew or chowder.

MUSSELS are used as food in many countries and in some parts of the United States. Here, the East Coast mussels tend to grow in sheltered places where their beds come in contact with sewage. In California, where the mussels grow on the open coast, they often eat tiny sea life that is poisonous to human beings. Because of these two circumstances, mussels are not always safe to eat in America. Mussels that grow in waters that are clean and free from poisonous organisms provide delicious and valuable food.

There are thousands and thousands of pounds of mussels grown every year. They grow on rocks, on pilings, under piers, and in cracks on the bottoms of tide pools, usually in moderate and cool waters. The most common mussel is the Blue Mussel, whose empty shells can be found on nearly any beach. Other kinds are the very large Horse Mussel, the California Mussel, and the Atlantic Ribbed Mussel.

Mussels have an interesting way of attaching themselves to rocks, pilings, or to other mussels. They make tough threads with a gland in the foot. The gland secretes a thick, sticky liquid, which the foot directs from the animal's shell to the spot where it is to be fastened. The liquid hardens to a tough golden thread, called the byssus, ending in a hard disk on the rock or piling. Whenever a mussel has to move, it makes new threads and discards the old ones as the new are being made. Thus, it never really lets go. It shifts its position only slightly. In some mussel beds, the animals are packed together so tightly that any moving at all is impossible. Mussels grow and multiply at a very rapid rate.

Find a bunch of mussels on a piling or on a rock. Try to pry some loose. Examine the threads that hold them in place. Notice the way in which the threads serve as guy wires, holding the animal safely even when waves and tide dash against it. There are other bivalves that use threads in this same way, but mussels are the most common and hence the easiest for you to see and collect.

Live mussels

OYSTERS are probably the best known mollusks in the world. All through history, they have been prized as a delicious food. We eat all of the oyster's body (except its shell, of course!) and we eat oysters only in the months that have an "r" somewhere in the name. The months without an "r" — May, June, July, August — are the warm months of late spring and summer, the months when the oysters breed. During these months, experts believe that the oyster flesh is less delicious than in the cooler months.

Oysters move about even less than mussels do. In fact, after babyhood oysters cannot move at all except to open and close their shells. Their millions and millions of eggs hatch into larvae, which can move about freely. Each larva chooses a place for its future life, wipes the spot clean with its foot, and then covers the spot with a kind of waterproof cement made by a gland in its foot. It then attaches itself firmly by means of its own cement to a rock, root, or shell of an older oyster. As it grows, the oyster adds more cement to keep itself firmly attached. If the oyster is taken out of water, it closes its shell tightly, holding in enough water to keep itself alive for a long time.

Oysters may seem to have a calm and secure life. Indeed, we say, "As calm as an oyster" — but the truth is that the oyster has a life filled with dangers and enemies. Long before it is anchored down, the baby oyster may be eaten by any one of a number of meat-eating sea creatures. And throughout its life it is in danger of being drilled into by an oyster drill, forced open by a starfish, invaded by a crab, or smothered by a slipper limpet, which likes to settle down on an oyster's shell. And then there is man, always looking for fresh oysters to harvest for food. The oyster cannot escape its enemies. If an oyster really is calm, as the proverb suggests, it is probably because there is nothing it can do to escape or to defend itself.

When you pick up an empty oyster shell along the beach, look for scars that might tell you how the animal met its death. Get a fresh living oyster if you can. Get it either from the sea or from a fish market. You will find it very hard to open. Indeed, unless you have very strong muscles and just the right way of inserting a knife blade between the shell edges, you will not be able to open the oyster at all. If so, get help so that you can see what an oyster looks like while it is still attached to its shell.

CLAMS are burrowing animals that live in mud, sand, or even in such hard materials as wood and rock. Each clam can burrow only as deep as its siphons are long. It must always be able to stretch its siphons up to reach the water, which is its source of food and oxygen. Clams with long "necks" (in which the siphons are extended) can dig themselves fairly deep into the sand. Some clams can disappear into the sand faster than you can dig after them. A clam moves by extending its large foot, grasping the sand or mud, and then pulling its body and shell in after it.

When you examine an empty clam shell, notice the two large round marks on the inside. These spots mark the places where two groups of strong muscles were attached. These muscles opened and closed the two halves of the shell.

There are many, many kinds of clams. All of them are edible, though some are too tiny to be worth the trouble. The entire clam is eaten — foot, neck, mantle, internal organs, everything, just as in the case of an oyster. Many kinds of clams are protected by law. Only a certain number that meet a legal size may be taken at any one time. Some of the common clams are listed below.

Quahog or *Hard-Shell Clams* were known and eaten by the Indians of the East Coast. *Little Neck* and *Cherry Stone Clams* are small members of the same family. The inside of a quahog shell has a lovely pearly glow with a pattern of white and purple. Indians used this shell material for wampum beads. Quahogs are clams of the Atlantic Coast.

Little Necks of the Pacific Coast are the most common clams of the western shores. They are sometimes called *Rock Venus Clams*.

Pismo Clams, from the coast of California, are known all over for their delicious flavor.

Razor Clams are easily recognized by their shells, which look like old-fashioned straight razors. A razor clam, which is long and thin, usually lives in an up-and-down position with its foot pointing out of the lower end. The foot pushes into the sand, expands quickly, and pulls the rest of the clam downward. This is repeated over and over with great speed. The razor clam can burrow so fast that it is almost impossible to dig one out alive.

Razor clam

Soft-Shell Clams are found on both coasts, but are most numerous along the Atlantic. These clams live in shallow, muddy flats, where they can be dug out at low tide. Their shells are soft, dull, chalky white.

There are many other kinds of clams that are valued as food. There are also some members of the clam family that are nuisances and even harmful to man. One of these is the *Piddock* or *Rock-Boring Clam*, which can burrow and grind its way into moderately hard rock and even into concrete pilings.

If you are not near an ocean beach, you can still get some specimens of bivalve mollusks. There are a number of fresh-water clams and mussels. There are the *Pill Clams* and *Finger-nail Clams*, tiny fellows, about a half inch long. They are active mollusks and do well in a fresh-water aquarium.

The larger fresh-water clams and mussels range from three to five inches in size. One kind, the *Washboard Mussel*, has wavy ridges across its shell from the hinge side to the edge. This is the kind of shell that makes the best pearl buttons, which are cut from the mother-of-pearl. Other mussels commonly found in ponds, lakes, and streams are *Maple Leaf, Fat Mucket, Elk Toe,* and *Floater*. Most of these are brown or greenish-brown on the outside. The *Fat Mucket*, however, is a shiny yellow.

While some of these fresh-water mollusks are called mussels, they live and behave much as the sea clams do, burrowing in the mud or sand, and moving about with the aid of a broad, muscular foot.

SCALLOPS, also known as PECTINS, are among the most beautiful and interesting of all the common bivalves you will find. They live in shallow to moderately deep salt water, usually resting on a sandy bottom. We eat only the large, single muscle that holds the shell together. The rest of the animal is thrown away, though people who have eaten the entire animal say that it is as delicious as an oyster.

The two halves of the scallop's shell are not exactly the same shape. One half is always deeper, more bowl-shaped than the other half. The flatter half is the part that is on top when the animal swims or lies on the bottom.

All around the edge of the mantle and sticking out of the shell like a fringe are fine hairlike tentacles. These help the animal to protect itself from tiny enemies that might try to enter its shell. The edge of the mantle has another feature that makes the scallop different from other bivalves. It has eyes, thirty to forty of them, bright blue, which peer out from under the edge of its shell. It can sense quick movements near it and can react to light and shadow.

Not only does the scallop have sight, but it also has the ability to move fast and so get away from any dangers it senses. It can move swiftly through the water by opening and closing its shell — flap-flap, like a little bellows. It can also make quick movements in any direction by using the edge of its mantle to control the water that goes in and out, thus jet-propelling itself in times of danger.

Scallop shells, of course, have scallops around the edges. These scalloped edges are the result of heavy ribs that extend fanlike from the hinge to the edge of the shell. The ribs make the shell very strong. And when the two halves of the shell close, the ribs fit perfectly, thus making a tight closing that is very hard to force open.

Even if you should not be lucky enough to catch sight of a scallop in action, you should be able to find empty scallop

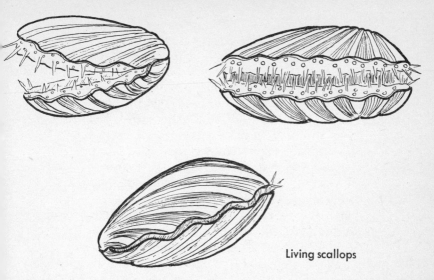

Living scallops

shells on most beaches. These lovely fan-shaped, ribbed, scallop-edged shells are not hard to recognize. They may also be recognized by their shell wings that stick out from the hinge side. These projections help to protect the animal's siphon. Usually the wings are unequal in size. The shells themselves vary from under an inch to more than six inches across and may be golden tan, rosy pink, creamy white, or decorated with striped or mottled designs. A single perfect scallop shell is as beautiful as anything you can own.

JINGLE SHELLS are thin, delicate, golden shells. They are almost transparent. The bivalves that make them spend their lives anchored to the backs of oysters or to underwater rocks. They glue themselves down, and their flat bottom shells are rarely torn loose. The jingle shells you find tossed on the beach are just the top shells of the animal. As the mollusk dies, its flesh lets go of its top shell. Because jingle shells are unusually light in weight, large numbers of them are carried ashore by waves and tide.

SHIPWORMS are not worms at all, but worm-shaped bivalves. They are destructive animals that have been causing damage to ships, bridges, and pilings all through history. And while man has fought the shipworm for hundreds and hundreds of years, the shipworm seems always to survive and continue its way of life, which is boring into wood and living in the burrows it makes. The way in which this small mollusk is able to drill through solid wood is quite a wonderful process. First of all, the shipworm enters the wood when it is a larva. As it grows, it develops a pair of small wing-shaped shells at the foot end. The foot and the shells are moved around and back, around and back, about ten times a minute. Gradually, a perfectly round tunnel is made. This is the burrow in which the animal will live. Many shipworms tunnel into a single piece of wood, in pilings, on the bottoms of boats, and in any other wood that is under water. When wood is completely filled with shipworm tunnels, it suddenly collapses. In your exploring trips along the seashore, look at pilings under wharfs and at other wood structures that extend below the water line. Hunt for evidence of shipworms. Perhaps you can find some driftwood that is filled with smooth round tunnels. If so, keep it as part of your shell collection and label it, "EMPTY BURROWS MADE BY SHIPWORMS (Bivalve Mollusks)."

There are many, many more bivalves, some of them common and some of them rare, and some of them found only in certain areas. You may find *Ark Shells, Sea Pens, Pandora Shells, Chestnut Clams, Lucinas, Cockles, Macomas, Angel Wings, Tellins,* and others. You will recognize them as bivalves, and if you want to identify them, you can look them up in shell books from the library.

Bivalves and univalves are not the only kinds of mollusks. They are the two main groups, the groups that include most of the mollusks you are likely to find. But you may want to know what other groups of mollusks are known. Scientists list three other groups.

CHITONS, a class all to themselves, are the most primitive of all mollusks. Chitons are commonly found along the Pacific Coast, and less commonly on the Atlantic. The animal has a shell made of tight, overlapping plates. It has a powerful foot with which it clings to rocks, holding so tightly that it can be pried loose only by working a thin knife blade between the

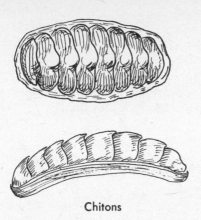

Chitons

foot and the rock. Once a chiton is detached from the security of its rock, it will protect itself by curling up so that its armor-like plates cover its entire body. Dead shells are washed ashore with the plates still connected to each other or with each of the shell plates separate. Each plate is shaped like the wings of a tiny butterfly and is often a lovely pearly sea blue on its inner surface.

TUSK SHELLS form another class of mollusks. These sea animals have bodies enclosed in a single tubelike shell, which is open at both ends. They have delicate tentacles, a mouth, and a single foot, all emerging from the large end of the shell. They have no definite head. Tusk shells are found on both the Atlantic and the Pacific coasts.

The fifth class of mollusks includes the SQUID, DEVILFISH, CUTTLEFISH, OCTOPUS, and NAUTILUS. These ocean creatures all have big heads, large eyes, and radulas. Instead of a single foot, each animal has eight to ten tentacles. Some of them, like the nautilus, have shells on the outside. Some, like the cuttle-fish, have small internal shells. And others, like the squid and octopus, have no shell at all, at least not in their adult stages, But when they are very, very young, these shell-less mollusks begin to grow shells. The shells stop growing after a while, and gradually the tiny shells practically disappear in the full-grown bodies.

As you become better acquainted with mollusks, through collecting and identifying their beautiful shells and through observing the living shell makers, you will notice how different living things are dependent upon each other. Later, in Chapter Seventeen, when you explore a tide-pool community, you will discover more things about mollusk families — what they look like, how they live, and how they die.

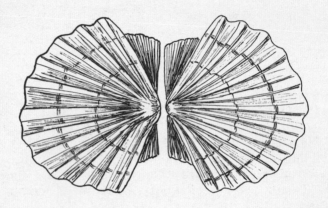

Two valves of a scallop shell

NINE

Starfish and Their Relatives

Starfish and their relatives form a group of animals called echinoderms. Echinoderm means "spiny-skin." Starfish and other echinoderms have plates of hard or prickly or spiny material covering and protecting the soft parts of their bodies. These animals could just as truthfully be called "starforms," because all of them in the adult stage have bodies that show a definite star pattern. As you meet the echinoderms, see how many different kinds of star shapes you can discover.

Of all the echinoderms in the world (between five and six thousand kinds) there are none at all that live in fresh water. They are all salt-water, or marine, animals. So, to observe and experiment with live starfish, you will have to explore the rocks, tide pools, and beaches beside the ocean. You will never discover any echinoderms on fresh-water banks or shores. But even if you have never seen the ocean, you probably know what starfish look like. The common five-armed starfish is often used in pictures and designs to create a marine atmosphere. Dried starfish are often sold as novelties or for use as decorations. They are unusual and attractive-looking, and many people think of them as valuable and desirable sea animals. It is true that they are interesting, even remarkable creatures in many ways. But, because of their taste for oysters and their unusual skill at satisfying this taste, starfish are destructive nuisances. However, it is their nature to eat bivalves. Their remarkable bodies that enable them to do this make them fascinating animals to observe.

A starfish has no head or tail, and no right or left side. It has only a top and bottom, with its arms or rays growing out from a central disc like the spokes of a wheel. There are many kinds of starfish. The most common kind has five arms. Others have ten or more arms, usually in multiples of five. On the underside of each arm there are little suction cups that enable the animal to hold tightly to solid surfaces. A starfish can "walk" up a vertical wall, hold fast to rocks even in strong seas, and get a death grip on the shells of oysters and other mollusks. The suction cups are operated by means of a water system inside the animal's body.

If you have a common five-ray starfish to examine, look first at its top surface. You will find, near the center, a spot that looks as though it might be a single eye. It is not an eye, but an opening for water. The opening is covered by a sieve plate, which is a kind of filter. This unusual opening is part of a special water system that makes it possible for the starfish to develop powerful suction. This is the way the system works. Water enters the starfish's body through the sieve plate. It is then piped through special water tubes that run like a plumbing system to the arms. On the bottom of each arm are many little tube feet, which lie in rows. Each of these little tube feet is filled with water from the water system. When the animal

Water system of a starfish

suddenly draws the water out of its tube feet, a suction is created. When the water is allowed to flow back into the tube feet, the suction is broken.

It is this water-suction system that gives the starfish its power over bivalve mollusks. A relatively small five-ray star-fish can force open a large oyster shell. The oyster, in spite of its strong, tough muscle hinge, cannot defend itself from a star-fish's attack. The starfish wraps its rays around the oyster and fastens its tube feet tightly to the shell. With the suction-cup tube feet on both halves of the bivalve, the starfish begins to exert pressure. Scientists have watched and experimented with starfish in order to discover how they are able to force open the strong-muscled oysters. First of all, a starfish of average size can pull with about three pounds of pressure. By means of its suction system, the starfish can hold on and keep up a steady pressure. In order to do this, it humps up its body and pulls the two shell halves in opposite directions.

Probably the starfish uses more than the force of its pull to open the oyster. Scientists now think that as soon as the oyster opens its shell a tiny crack, the starfish gives it a shot of some chemical to relax its muscles. The chemical is made in the starfish's body and is probably poured out through its mouth, which is held against the side of the shell that is opening. Once the oyster's shell muscles relax, the shells can be opened easily. The next part of the attack is equally unusual.

The starfish's purpose for getting the oyster to open its shell is, of course, to eat the soft body of the oyster. But remember the position the starfish is in. It is using at least four of its arms to hold the oyster's shell open. If the pressure is relaxed the oyster may close its shell again. How, then, can the starfish get the oyster's body out of the shell and into its own stomach? The starfish solves this problem in a most unusual way. Its mouth is on its underside, right in the middle. Its mouth is already against the open edge of the shell. It now turns part of its stomach inside out, through its mouth. The stomach pours digestive juices over the oyster flesh, partly digesting it outside the body of the starfish. As soon as the starfish finishes its meal, it draws its stomach back inside and moves on, possibly to seek another bivalve meal.

Starfish prey on oyster beds, and also help themselves to clams, mussels, and other bivalves. Some kinds of starfish will also eat univalves. Starfish destroy millions of dollars worth of mollusks each year. A single starfish has been known to eat as many as ten oysters or clams in a day. No wonder, then, that a horde of starfish swarming over a bed of oysters can wipe it out overnight.

There are several ways in which starfish populations are controlled. In some oyster-raising places, the oyster beds are swept with long, long mops. The mops are made of bunches of long strings. As the strings move over them, many of the starfish grab them with their tube feet and hang on. Then the mops are lifted out of the water and the starfish that are caught in the strands are destroyed. Another way of getting rid of starfish is to spread a chemical over the oyster beds. The chemical (quicklime) can be made just strong enough to kill the starfish without hurting the oysters. Recently, scientists who work for the United States Fish and Wildlife Service have suggested that oyster beds would be better off in bays and harbors than they are along the open coast. Inshore waters are less salty than the waters in the open sea. Oysters do well where there is less salt, but starfish must have very salty water in order to thrive. Meanwhile, scientists are working on a chemical screen against starfish. A sort of chemical wall will be placed around the oyster beds. This, it is hoped, will form a barrier that no starfish can cross.

Oyster fishermen used to try to destroy starfish by tearing up the ones they caught and throwing them back into the sea. But this is no longer done because it is now known that if a starfish is torn into two parts, each part may grow into a whole animal. In fact, there are some kinds of starfish that can actually break themselves into parts and grow each part into a new starfish! Usually, with the common five-ray starfish you are most likely to see, a lost ray will be replaced by a new ray, which grows out from the central disc. And, if the broken ray or arm has enough of the central disc still with it, that single ray can grow into a whole new starfish!

This remarkable ability to grow back parts that are broken off, and to grow whole bodies from parts of bodies, is called the power of regeneration. Our bodies have some powers of regeneration. Fingernails and hair can be cut off all of our lives, and still our hair and nails continue to grow. Our skin, too, and many inside parts of our bodies can replace or regenerate themselves. But if a finger, of a leg, or an ear is cut off, it cannot be regrown. The human body, and the bodies of other highly developed animals, have very limited powers of regeneration compared with those of the starfish.

Common starfish   Starfish regenerating two rays

You probably cannot do any experiments with starfish regeneration. In order to regrow missing parts, the animal has to be in a proper sea-water environment. If you try to divide a starfish in half in order to grow two starfish, you are likely to end up with two pieces of very dead starfish. (Later, as described in Chapter Ten, you will be doing some experimenting in regeneration, though not with starfish.)

What you can do now is to search for starfish that are in the process of regrowing missing parts. Look for starfish on the beach after a storm, in tide pools, under bunches of seaweed, and on the underwater parts of piers and wharfs, where the starfish are likely to gather to feed on mussels. Examine each starfish you find. If some rays are smaller than the others, it is because the small ones are being regenerated. You may find a specimen with three good rays and two little stumps where the other rays ought to be. In time, the stumps will grow into full-sized rays. Or you may find a specimen with one large ray, a small central disc, and four little budding rays. Such an animal is regrowing a complete body from a single ray.

If you touch a starfish while it is in the water, it will feel firm and muscular. Out of water, however, it will become soft and limp. This is because the water leaks out through its tube feet and is not being replaced, since the sieve plate is out of water. Starfish breathe oxygen from the water and cannot live long on land. Do your examining and experimenting in the water. Turn a starfish over on its back (its top side) and watch the way it uses its rays to work itself right side up. Then, notice the way in which it moves across a pebbly or sandy surface. One ray will lead the way, while the other four will be used, two by two, like legs. When the starfish changes its direction, another ray will point the way, and again the other four will serve as legs. You can watch the "walking" patterns of a starfish for hours at a time and marvel at the ease with which it changes direction and pairs up its rays.

As you look at the rays, you may notice a small red eyespot on the end of each one. These dots are not real eyes, but they provide the only means of seeing that a starfish has. The eyespots let the animal know light from dark, and that is about all. But near the eyespots are areas for the sense of smell. A starfish can smell its food much more easily than it can see it. Here is an experiment you can do with a piece of oyster or clam meat.

Tie some strong thread around a bit of oyster or clam meat and fasten it to a short stick. Drop the meat into the water near a starfish. Dangle the bait near the tips of the animal's rays. If the starfish is at all hungry, it will follow the meat as you trail it through the water. Remember, it is doing this because it *smells* the food, not because it can see it. After you have tested the animal's response to the smell of food, untie the bait and leave it on a stone where the starfish can capture and eat it.

Starfish reproduce in two main ways. They lay eggs, which hatch into tiny larvae. The larvae swim around for a few weeks and then change into tiny, tiny starfish. Many die in these early stages. Only those that escape the many large, hungry sea animals can finally reach some area where there are plenty of mollusks to eat. A second way of reproducing is by regeneration. Some kinds of starfish actually break themselves into five equal parts. Each of the five rays moves off on its own and grows itself a whole new body. There are always more than enough starfish, and they can be found on all coasts. The common five-ray starfish is red or purplish in color. There are other kinds of starfish. You may be lucky enough to discover some of the less common ones listed below.

Sun Star is a large animal, sixteen to twenty inches across. It has ten rays and is found on the Atlantic Coast.

Sunflower Star is similar to the sun star except that it has twice as many rays and is on the Pacific Coast. It sometimes gets to be thirty inches across.

Brittle Star has five long, thin, snakelike arms, which are loosely fastened to a central disc. Sometimes the center is round. Sometimes it is five-sided. Brittle stars are hard to catch because they can easily detach any arm you might try to hold on to. The ease with which the arms can be broken off has given this animal its name. Look for little brittle stars in the tangles of seaweed that are left on the beach as the tide goes out. You may find some that are only an inch or two across. Others are often as large as five inches across.

Basket Star looks like a kind of basket. It has five branching arms growing out from a five-sided center. Each of the branches makes more branches, like those of a tree. These branching arms are used for curling around rocks or holding the animal to a clump of seaweed.

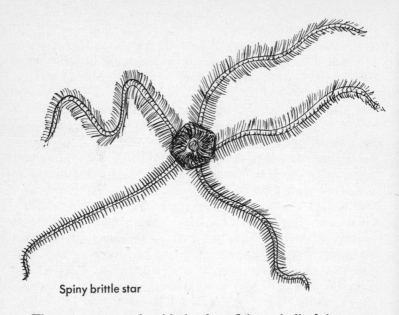

Spiny brittle star

There are many other kinds of starfish, and all of them seem to be built on some sort of five-point plan. The starfish relatives, too, have a characteristic star pattern, though in some cases you have to look carefully in order to find it.

SEA URCHINS do not look at all like starfish. They look more like little puffballs covered with brightly colored porcupine quills. The quills, or spines, stick out in all directions. The animals are red, green, purple, or black and often form a living carpet on the bottom of the sea. Do not step on a sea urchin, for some of them have tiny poison cells that can give you a painful sting.

Among its spines, the sea urchin has five double rows of tube feet, which it uses to move itself along on the sea bed. No matter how it falls, it always has some of its tube feet in a position to help itself get right side up. Its spines are movable, and they, as well as its tube feet, help it to move around. The spines act as stilts and can keep the animal raised from the ocean floor. Unlike its starfish cousin, the sea urchin is mainly a plant eater. It feeds on plants that cling to rocks or float in the sea. It is able to scrape crusts of algae from the rocks by using its five pointed teeth, located in its mouth in the middle of its underside.

Look for live sea urchins in protected places near shore, clinging to ledges, holding to the undersides of rocks, and in various cracks and caves where the action of waves will not wash them away. They live on the Atlantic and Pacific coasts.

The hollow shells, or tests, of sea urchins are sometimes found on the beach. When you examine one of these tests, you will see clearly the relationship to the starfish family. Running from the hole on the underside (the mouth opening) to the middle of the top are five rays, each with a double row of tiny openings. The animal's tube feet stuck out through these openings. All over the test are little bumps, to which the spines were attached. Empty tests of dead sea urchins are easily broken. If you can find some for your seashore collection, be sure to protect them in a bed of cotton or tissue.

Test of a sea urchin

Live sea urchin

SAND DOLLARS, close relatives of sea urchins, are other interesting members of the spiny-skinned group. On a sand dollar, the spines are movable, but so soft and fine that the animal seems to be covered with velvet. It uses its spines (rather than its tiny tube feet) to help it move from place to place. Sand dollars live half buried in sand or mud, usually in fairly deep water. They feed on plankton and other small organic materials.

It is not likely that you will discover a living sand dollar, but you are almost certain to run across some of the empty shells, or tests, that are washed up on the beach. By studying a sand dollar test, you can learn something about the living animal. On the top surface you will see the typical five-ray pattern, in this case looking like the outline of a flower with five petals. This shows where the two rows of tiny tube feet stuck out. Turn the test over and notice the five marks on the underside. These grooves were used by the living animal to help pass food along to its mouth, which was in the middle of its underside. Shake the sand dollar test. Do you hear something rattle inside? If you have several empty tests to experiment with, break one open. Inside, you will find the remains of the animal's five teeth. Examine them with your hand lens. If the test has not been worn away too much by sand and sea, you may be able to see clearly the animal's chewing parts.

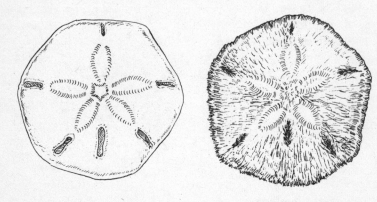

Test of a sand dollar   Live sand dollar

SEA CUCUMBERS are soft and shaped like cucumbers. They live in fairly cool water on both the Atlantic and Pacific Coasts. They live on rocky shores under rock ledges below the low-tide level. Their tube feet are arranged along the sides of their bodies in a five-ray pattern. At one end of a sea cucumber is its mouth, surrounded by a ring of tentacles. The animal looks like a strange-colored cucumber with a fringe on top. It may be reddish brown, black, white, or sand colored. It has no hard shell covering, its only protection being a tough, leathery skin and an unusual way of escaping its enemies. If it is attacked by a hungry creature, the sea cucumber can push out its own insides. While its enemy is busy eating this soft material, the rest of the animal, mainly its empty skin, drifts off to a safe place. Then, with its special power of regeneration, it can actually grow itself a whole new set of internal organs!

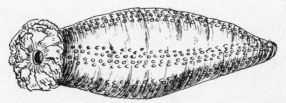

Sea cucumber

As you wade in the shallow water along a rocky shore or explore the living things in a tide pool, look for the colorful and interesting echinoderms. See how many different kinds and colors you can discover in your area. If you get a chance, examine some of them through your magnifying glass. Fill a pail with sea water. Better yet, use a large glass bowl, if you have one handy. Then if you can catch a sea urchin, starfish, or other member of this interesting group, pick it up with your kitchen-strainer scoop and place it in your container of sea water. This will give you a chance to examine the animal carefully from all angles and to make sketches of it if you wish. When you have explored one creature, return it to its ocean home. Then get fresh sea water and look for another specimen to study in the same way.

TEN

Water Worms

What is a worm? Many of the things we call worms are not worms at all. Silkworms and the worms in apples are insects in the larva stage. True worms are not insects and do not change into insects or into anything else. They are a separate kind of soft-bodied animal without a skeleton. They are usually much longer than they are wide; they move in a crawling motion; and they have only their skins to protect the soft parts of their bodies.

One way of classifying worms is by the form of their bodies — flat, round, or in sections. Thus we have flatworms, roundworms, and segmented worms. Scientists know of about twenty *thousand* different kinds of worms in these three classes! Some of them are useful, helpful, or valuable to man. Others are harmful, annoying, or dangerous. Some are beautiful to look at and others are repulsive. Some live in water, some in the soil, and some (the parasites) live in the bodies of other animals. Of the waterworms, some live only in the fresh waters of lakes, ponds, and streams. Others are marine, or ocean, creatures.

FLATWORMS. Among the worms you can find along the seashore are several kinds of flatworms. All flatworms are carnivorous, or meat-eating. They feed on other worms, eggs, larvae, and other living things. They like to catch their food alive. You can find flatworms clinging to the undersides of rocks under water along the shore. Some are yellow, some brown, some gray, and some are striped. There are some flatworms that take their color from the last meal they have eaten. Their skins are very thin, and a meal of pink meat will make them pink while purple food will turn them purple. On the Pacific

Coast there are some flatworms that are an inch and a half long and nearly as wide. They are beautifully colored and beautifully marked. You can find them under large rocks resting on damp, but not wet, gravel.

Flatworms are the simplest, most primitive of the three kinds of worms. Their heads are at one end, and their mouths are in the middle of their undersides, opening directly into their stomachs. There is a kind of frilly tube around the mouth. When a flatworm eats, it can settle on its food, surrounding it with its mouth tube. It can then pour digestive juices over the food and, as it is digested, suck it up into the stomach. Flatworms are able to glide over surfaces. Most of them can also swim, using a rippling movement of their bodies for locomotion. You will discover more about flatworms later as you collect and experiment with fresh-water flatworms.

RIBBON WORMS. Most ribbon worms are found in sea water. This kind of worm is very, very long, twenty feet or more, with a mouth at one end and an intestine running all the way through its body. It swims at night and by day lives in mud and under rocks. It eats worms and other small sea creatures.

The ribbon worm is especially fond of segmented worms. If you tie a string around a segmented worm and trail it in front of a ribbon worm, you may see an interesting demonstration of how food is tracked, captured, and eaten. First of all, a special nose tube will come shooting out from an opening in the side of the ribbon worm's head. With this tube, called a proboscis, the worm will track its prey. When close enough, it will strike with the pointed end of the proboscis, then wrap the proboscis around the body of the dying segmented worm, and finally eat it.

Ribbon worm

Ribbon worms and flatworms have remarkable powers of regeneration. They can regrow any parts of their bodies that are broken off. And, if their bodies are cut into a number of pieces, each piece can grow into a complete individual.

The most advanced worms are the segmented ones. Their bodies are made up of a series of segments or rings. The common earthworms you find in your garden are of this type, but most of the segmented worms of the world live in the sea. Below are some of the interesting ones to look for as you explore the seashore.

CLAM WORMS. One of the largest and most common of all marine worms is the clam worm. It is blue-green or reddish in color, often with an iridescent shine. Its thick body sometimes reaches a length of fifteen to eighteen inches. It hunts and feeds on small mollusks and other sea creatures. You can find clam worms in the daytime in their mucus-lined sand burrows below the low-tide level. At night they leave their holes and swim around in search of food.

Clam worm

PARCHMENT WORMS. The parchment worm gets its name from the tough, leathery skin with which it lines its U-shaped burrow. The tube may be as long as two feet, and as thick as an inch around. But the ends that stick up are only about half as wide as the underground part of the tube. Look for the tube chimneys in the sandy mud below low-tide level. Watch also for empty tubes, which are sometimes washed up by the waves.

Parchment worms use their unusual tubes to bring them oxygen and food. Water is sucked in at one end of the tube and pushed out at the other end. The worm gets oxygen and tiny plankton creatures from the water that it draws through its tube.

There are many other kinds of tube worms in the sea. Some of them have delicate, feathery tentacles in beautiful colors. They look like fantastic flowers as they gather food by waving their exquisite tentacles to and fro in the water. Each worm is encased in a limy tube or in a tube made of mud and sand, cemented together by a material formed in its own body.

If you happen to see one of these beautiful, flower-like worms, pick it up and place it in a glass jar filled with sea water. Keep the water cool as you study the worm through your magnifying glass. Some tube worms are among the most strikingly beautiful of all sea creatures.

LUGWORMS. A segmented worm that is much like our common earthworm is the thick, rather ugly lugworm. It lives in burrows in the sand just below the low-water mark. It gathers sand and other loose material on its sticky funnel-shaped proboscis, which is then drawn into its mouth. The material is swallowed, passed through its intestine, and the parts that cannot be digested are passed out as casts. When the tide is going out, you may see little piles of sandy casts beside the burrows. If you dig down, you can usually find a lugworm in its hole. Fishermen dig for lugworms to use as bait.

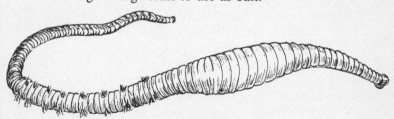

Lugworm

Compared with the large and colorful worms of the sea, the fresh-water worms may seem rather unimportant. They are small and drab, but some of them have most interesting life histories. And since they live in fresh water, they can be captured and kept in small glass-jar aquariums for careful observation. In fact, if you made a miniature aquarium as discussed in Chapter Five, you may have seen some of the fresh-water worms described below.

HAIRWORMS. A hairworm looks like a piece of very fine, wiry horsehair. You may dig one up in mud you scoop from the bottom of a pond. Put the mud into a jar, fill the jar with pond water, and watch for the twisting and coiling movements of the hairworm as the water clears. Lift the hairworm out of the water for a moment and stretch it out full length. You will be surprised to find that this tiny, tangled, wriggling mass is a foot or more long. After measuring it, put it back into the jar of water and watch it through your magnifying glass.

Hairworms lay their eggs in blobs of jelly. The eggs hatch into tiny larvae, which bore their way into the bodies of water insects. There they grow into adults. Then they leave the insects' bodies and return to the water to find mates and lay eggs.

Any animal that lives on or in the body of another animal is called a parasite. The larvae of hairworms, then, are parasites. They get their food from the host animals, the ones in which they live. Many of the hairworm larvae never manage to get back to their water home. But there are always enough that do to keep the ponds and streams well stocked with adult hairworms and their eggs.

LEECHES. Leeches are among the most interesting of all the boneless creatures that live in our fresh waters. They fairly swarm in ditches, lakes, ponds, and slow-flowing streams. Most kinds of leeches prefer quiet and fairly warm water and plenty of shade or darkness.

A leech is a segmented worm with a body that is somewhat fatter in the middle than on the ends. At one end is a suction cup with which the animal attaches itself to a rock, a stone, or to another animal. At the other end, the leech has a sucking mouth with which to draw blood from other creatures. Small leeches feed upon little snails, worms, turtles, and other small water animals. Larger leeches attach themselves to large water creatures and to the legs of wading animals. A leech will draw out as much blood as it can hold and then drop off. After a good full meal, a leech does not need to eat again for weeks or even for months.

In your miniature aquarium you may find a few of the small brown or black worm leeches. These are slim and may be a half inch or less in length. But their bodies are so elastic that you can stretch them out to more than an inch. If you have any leeches in your aquarium, try feeding them a tiny, tiny bit of raw liver. The bloodier, the better. The raw blood will usually attract a leech, which will wave its mouth end toward it. It will attach its sucking mouth to the liver and draw a meal of blood from it. Then it will live, quietly digesting its meal, for a long time without eating.

PLANARIANS. A common fresh-water flatworm is the planaria. Planarians live under dead leaves and on the surface of stones on the bottom of quiet streams and ponds. They like cool, shaded places. They glide along under the water by contracting and expanding their body muscles. They can be found in most quiet bodies of fresh water. You may have dug up one or more of them with the mud and stones and plant material you used for your miniature aquarium. Hunt for them carefully. You should be able to see them without using your magnifying glass. Below are listed some of the common kinds of planarians to look for.

Large black flatworm, one inch or more in length
Large white flatworm, one inch or more in length (less common)
Small black flatworm, only one-fourth of an inch long
Chain flatworm, transparent, only one-fourth of an inch long; often several small flatworms of this type fastened together in chain style

Planarians are of great interest to scientists because of their special ability to regrow, or regenerate, whole bodies from a small part. Here are some experiments you can do with planarians.

First of all, catch some planarians in the slow-moving waters of a stream or in the shallows of a pond or lake among the water weeds. To attract the worms, use a two-inch cube of raw beef or liver tied with a string and dangled among the water plants for an hour or so. When you pull in the meat, it will likely be covered with flatworms of various sizes and colors.

If you live where you cannot catch your specimens in a natural pond or stream, you may be able to get some from an aquarium dealer in a pet store. Planarians often come in on shipments of fresh-water plants that aquarium dealers buy from the growers. If an aquarium dealer has any among his water plants, he will probably be glad to give you a jarful of water with a few of them in it. Be sure, though, to bring your own jar and cover. Keep your largest planarians in a glass jar filled with water from the stream, pond, or the aquarium from which they came. Put a piece of meat or liver in the jar, too. The worms will gorge themselves on it and will then not need to eat for days or weeks. In fact, when planarians cannot get any food at all, they can still keep alive for a long time. They simply live off their own bodies, actually absorbing themselves as they do so. In an experiment, some flatworms that were originally about a half inch long were kept away from food for nearly half a year. During that time they got smaller and smaller but did not die. When they were finally fed again, they rather quickly became their normal size. If you try this experiment, you will have to keep each planaria in a private bottle or jar. If you keep several of them together in a single jar, you can well imagine what may happen. One big fellow is likely to break its fast by eating up its companions! However, as long as you keep feeding your planarians, you can keep a number of them together in the same jar.

As your specimens make themselves at home, eating and moving around on the sides and bottom of the jar, you will have an excellent opportunity to study them through your hand lens. A planaria is said to be the lowest (or most simple) animal form that has a head, a right and left side, a front and back, a top and bottom, and something like a brain. Watch one of them as it moves smoothly around on the glass sides of the jar. As it moves, it stretches itself out to full length, which may be twice as long as it appears when at rest. Its body is covered with tiny hairlike bits that probably help it to move along. Mainly, though, it moves by expanding and contracting the muscles that fill its soft body.

While the worm is moving on the glass, you can get a good view of its underside. Notice an oblong pattern right in the middle of this bottom side. This is the animal's mouth. When it eats, it extends a proboscis out through its mouth. A proboscis is a kind of soft, flexible snout. With its proboscis, the planaria covers its food with slime and then swallows it by drawing it right into its intestinal tract, which is connected to its mouth opening. When the worm is trying to swallow something large, it can use its proboscis to pour out digestive juices. These juices go to work on the food, and as bits are digested, they are sucked in. Since the mouth is the only opening to the digestive system, the particles of undigested matter are passed out through the mouth.

Planarians are sensitive to light and will retreat from it. If you shine a flashlight on them at night you can test their reactions. They will try to find a dark place in which to hide.

The most interesting experiment to perform is one in regeneration. Put one of your largest planarians into a shallow saucer filled with pond water. Add a bit of raw liver or red meat. If the worm is hungry, it will attach itself to the meat and eat enough to last it for weeks. As soon as it begins to stretch its body and move about, you can cut it into two pieces. Use a razor blade or a very sharp knife to make the cut. Cut it through the middle. Each half will glide away on its own as though nothing had happened. Scientists tell us that the cutting does not cause pain to the animal. In fact, in their natural lives planarians often divide into pieces as a way of reproduction. After having cut the animal into two halves, watch through your magnifying glass to see what happens. Keep a daily record of your observations. Use drawings as well as descriptions. If all goes well with your experiment, the regeneration will happen something like the following, which a junior scientist recorded in her home study of planarians.

First day, less than a half hour after the cutting, dark masses formed on the cut edges.

Fifth day, a thin, transparent tissue had formed, building up a head area on the tail piece and a tail area on the head piece.

Eighth day, a head, lighter in color than the original piece, had taken form. Two eyespots began to develop.

Tenth day, on the regenerating head, the pointed lobes were clearly developed. The eyespots seemed more fully developed. The tail had regenerated on the front half.

Sixteenth day, both pieces had fully regrown their missing halves. The two regenerated planarians were smaller than the original planarian.

Twentieth day, the two new planarians had grown to normal size, about the length of the original specimen.

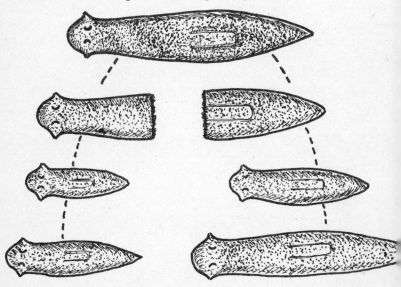

Regeneration of a planaria

The experiment can be repeated with these fast-growing fresh-water worms, making cuts of various sizes. A planaria cut into three pieces may grow into three new animals, and four pieces may grow into four. Under ideal conditions, a new planaria can grow from a very small piece.

Another experiment you can do is to see how a planaria can grow itself two complete heads. Select a large specimen for your experiment. Put it into a saucer or shallow glass dish. Keep the animal covered with pond water at all times. With a thin-edged razor blade, cut the head in half, lengthwise, extending the cut about a fourth of the way down the animal's body. Observe the new tissue forming and keep track of the number of days that pass until the animal has two perfectly formed heads on its single body.

Planarians are among the most interesting water animals to observe and experiment with, mainly because of their special ability to regrow missing parts and to develop whole bodies from tiny fragments. This is something that the higher forms of animal life are not able to do.

ELEVEN

Crusty Crustaceans

Crustaceans are animals that wear their skeletons on the outside of their bodies. They are covered with crusty, leatherlike armor, which does not grow as their bodies get bigger. When the shell becomes too small, it splits open and the animal crawls out of it. This is called molting. After molting, the crustacean's body is soft and unprotected. But a new shell gradually develops and hardens. This shell lasts until it, in turn, becomes too small, and then the animal molts again. Some crustaceans molt more than a dozen times during their lives.

Crustaceans, like many of the mollusks, have blood that is pale blue. The color is caused by a copper mineral. Human beings and many other kinds of animals have iron rather than copper in their blood. Iron makes blood red.

Most crustaceans are gill breathers and live in water, especially in the sea. They all have jointed legs. Some of them have large claws on their front legs. You are sure to know at least the three kinds of crustaceans that are important foods for man — lobster, crab, and shrimp. Still more important is the enormous number of crustaceans that serve as food for fish and other water animals. Tiny crustaceans, as you remember from Chapter Five, form an essential link in the food chain that goes on continuously in fresh waters and in the sea.

Below are described some of the common, easy-to-find crustaceans. Look for them on the beach at the seashore, in shallow tide pools, and on rocks at low tide.

SAND BUGS. If you have ever gone wading on a sandy beach beside either the Atlantic or the Pacific, you have probably noticed the sand bugs. Perhaps, when you were little, you used to scoop some of them up with your toy sand shovel and keep them imprisoned in your sand pail. It is always fun to see how fast these little sand bugs can disappear in the sand.

Sand bugs, of course, are not bugs at all. They are sometimes called mole crabs, but they are not true crabs, either. They are marine crustaceans, shaped something like little lobsters with their tails tucked under. The next time you go to the seashore, capture a sand bug in a glass jar with about an inch of fine sand on the bottom and enough sea water to cover the sand. Then tip the jar to one side so that the sand bug is out of the water. Watch through your magnifying glass as the animal quickly digs itself into the sand. Then tip the jar again and watch the sand bug come out of its temporary burrow in search of food.

Sand bugs feed on the tiny bits of sea life found in the water. They gather their food with their long, feathery antennae, as they are carried along on the edge of a wave. When the wave goes back, the sand bug quickly digs itself into the wet sand and stays there until the next wave reaches it and brings in more food. As you watch these interesting crustaceans, you will notice that all of their movements are backward. Swimming, walking, and digging are all done hind part first.

Sand bug

CRABS. In most places, you do not have to wander along the beach very long before you see a crab or two. There are many kinds of crabs. Some of them seem stupid, some timid, some busy — and all of them, for some reason, quite amusing. They hide under stones, scurry sideways behind a rock or piece of seaweed, draw themselves safely into burrows in the sand, or roam the beaches, especially at night. They form a kind of clean-up squad, as they feed upon dead and dying sea creatures. There are crabs that eat sea urchins, sea cucumbers, bivalve mollusks, and fish as well as algae and other plant life. Some crabs seem to be fussy about what they eat while others will eat practically anything. If you want to tempt a crab with some food, get a piece of mussel and place it in front of the crab, just back of its largest claws. If it is hungry, it will show you how it eats.

If you can catch a crab, put it into a glass bowl or an enamel pan while you examine it through your magnifying glass. Notice its two eyes at the end of stalks. Like periscopes, these can be raised and turned in any direction, thus giving the crab a good look around.

Look next for the crab's tail. To do this, you will have to turn the crab on its back. The tail is a small triangular piece that is held tightly against the underside of its body. With your fingers, pull it gently away from the body. You will see then that it is a true tail, connected to the end of the animal's back. The tail does not help it to swim, crawl, or dig, but for a female crab the tail has a very special purpose. It is used as a safe cradle for holding and carrying eggs. As the eggs are laid, they are fastened to the underside of the tail by a special kind of glue. As more and more eggs are laid, the tail is pushed away from the body, and the space between the tail and body serves as an egg pounch. The eggs hatch into tiny larvae, which look much like the larvae of oysters. Millions of free-swimming crab larvae are eaten up by hungry fish. The larvae that are not eaten grow into little crabs.

When a crab is ready to molt, a split forms across the back end of its shell, just where the tail begins to turn under. As the split gets wide enough, the crab begins to back out of its shell.

Its body, legs, mouth parts, and feelers are all drawn out of the old shell. Even the lining of its stomach is shed with the shell. As soon as the old shell is off, the crab's body quickly expands to a new, larger size. As soon as a crab molts, or loses its old shell, a new shell begins to form. Some crabs eat their old, discarded shells. In this way these crabs get extra amounts of calcium and other chemicals that are used in the shell-making process. Until a crab's new shell has become hard enough to protect its soft body, it does little but hide, protecting itself from possible enemies.

Some kinds of crabs are considered to be especially delicious when they are in the soft-shell stage. Since this is a very brief time immediately after the shell has been shed, crab fishermen catch the adult crabs and keep them in cages until they molt. Then they are ready to be sold, fried, and eaten as "soft-shelled crabs." Little young crabs shed their shells every few weeks. As they grow larger and older, their growth slows down and they molt every month or so. Full-grown adults usually molt only once a year.

As you walk along the beach, you will see discarded shells. You can gather these for your seashore collection. To discover whether an empty crab shell is a molt or the shell of a dead crab, lift off the top part of the shell. If it is a molt, you will find the cast of the gills on each side. You will also notice the lining of the stomach. Examine the lining and find the stomach teeth, with which the crab "chews" the food it has already swallowed. If the shell you find is the remains of a dead crab, there will be no slit along the back end, and inside you will see bits of flesh still clinging to the shell.

Crabs move along the ocean bottom and run across the sand in a sideways direction. The way their legs are formed makes it easier for them to do this than to move straight ahead. Only some crabs are able to swim. The swimmers have a hind pair of legs that are flattened at the ends like little paddles. Other crabs have hind legs ending in points, which help them to get a grip on rocks and to move easily over sand.

If a crab loses one of its legs, a new one slowly grows in its place. If part of a leg is destroyed, the entire leg is cast off at the base. From the base, a little bud, then a small limb, and finally, after months or even years of growth, a full-sized leg will replace the old one.

There are many, many kinds of crabs on both the Atlantic and Pacific shores. Here are some of the common kinds you are likely to see.

Hermit Crabs can be found on nearly all beaches. They have no hard shells over their abdomens. These soft rear parts are curved just right to fit into a univalve shell. A hermit crab hunts for an empty shell of the right size and backs into it. With its hind legs it hooks itself securely into the shell. Once inside, with its twisted body curved into the spiral shell and its hooklike tail anchoring it in place, the crab cannot easily be pulled out. Whenever a hermit crab grows too big for its borrowed shell, it finds a larger one and quickly shifts to its new home. Tiny hermits use shells that are only a fraction of an inch in size. Larger hermits use larger shells.

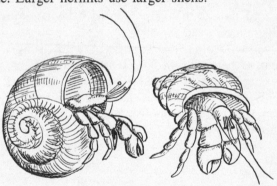

Hermit crabs in univalve shells

If you search in tide pools and among the pebbles on the beach at low tide, you can find periwinkles, moon shells, whelks, and other snail shells occupied by little hermit crabs. If you pick up one of these shells, the crab will protect itself by drawing back into the shell and closing the opening with its claws. But if you drop the shell into some cool sea water, the crab may relax enough to peek out and wave its claws around. Look at it through your magnifying glass. Notice its claws, feelers, and eye stalks. Hermit crabs are great scavengers. They will eat practically anything, especially meat. They will even eat other hermit crabs if they can catch them between shells.

Fiddler Crabs are burrowing animals. They live in long, slanting tunnels, which they build in the sand and line with mud. The entrance to a typical burrow lies just below the high-tide level. But before high tide is reached, the crab closes the entrance in order to prevent flooding of its home. Like all crabs, the fiddler is a true gill breather. But it can stay out of water for as long as six weeks at a time. When the water that it holds in its gill cavities is all used up, the fiddler will run sideways down to the edge of the sea and get more water. Then it can safely roam the beach again, picking out the bits of plant and animal material on which it feeds.

You can always recognize a male fiddler crab by its one oversized claw. This claw, usually the right one, is used mainly during the mating season, when the male waves it threatening-ly at another male. Whenever a male starts waving its huge claw around, its gestures make it look as though it is a fancy violin player. The big claw looks like a violin, or fiddle, and the little claw like a bow. Because of this amusing re-semblance, this kind of crab is called a fiddler.

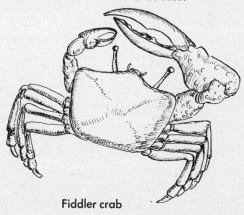

Fiddler crab

Once in a while a male will lose its big right claw in a fight. While the lost claw is slowly regenerating, the other one will quickly grow into a big claw. The new claw will become an ordinary small claw.

Sand or *Ghost Crabs*, like the fiddlers, dig burrows in sandy beaches and in salt marshes. They are the color of the white beaches where they often live. They scamper rapidly across the sand, moving in a quick, sideways direction, starting and stopping suddenly. They seem to disappear right before your eyes. This is why they are sometimes called ghost crabs.

Spider Crabs have pear-shaped bodies, narrow and pointed in front. The common kinds have unusually long, thin legs, which make them look like huge spiders. There are kinds of spider crabs in both the Atlantic and the Pacific. They live in shallow waters and are rather slow and sluggish in spite of their long legs. There are common spider crabs with bodies the size of a pear. There are also larger kinds, whose pear-shaped bodies are as long as a man's foot. The crusty backs of spider crabs are often covered with plant and animal growths — barnacles, algae, and other small organisms. The only way in which the crab can rid itself of these hitchhikers is to shed its entire shell at molting time.

Kelp Crabs are found among kelp beds and in tide pools along the Pacific Coast. They are close relatives of the spider crabs, but more active and with backs that are more free of foreign growth. Most kelp crabs are small and olive green. Their legs and bodies are sharp and spiny, and their claws are strong. They are able to cling to strands of seaweed even when the water is rough. They are also able to give you a sharp stab or pinch if you are careless in picking one up.

Blue Crabs are valuable members of the crab family. They are caught by the thousands and sold in sea-food markets. Some of them are sold just after they have molted, before the new shells have developed. They are the kind that is eaten as soft-shelled crab. Blue crabs are swimmers. When you see them, either on the beach or on the counter of a sea-food market, notice the way the hind pair of legs end in little paddles.

Blue crab, a swimmer

Green Crabs, Calico Crabs, and *Lady Crabs* are other swimming crabs, smaller and less important than blue crabs. Any
crab can be used as food. But those that are small have too little meat in them to be worth the trouble of catching and pre-
paring them.

HORSESHOE CRABS. A crablike animal that you may find
along the Atlantic beaches is called the horseshoe or king crab,
although it is not a crab at all. In fact, it is not even a crustacean. It belongs to an entirely different family, a family of
land creatures. Its closest relatives are the spiders. Horseshoe
crabs and their prehistoric ancestors have been on the earth
for several hundred million years and have changed very little
during all this time. For this reason they are sometimes called
living fossils.

The horseshoe crab has four pairs of walking legs and a
fifth pair of legs that is used to push its awkward body along
over the sand below the low-tide level. It has a large horseshoe-

shaped shell and a long spine for a tail. Its sharp tail is not used as a weapon. It is merely a handy spike that the animal digs into the sand in order to flip itself over whenever the waves have turned it on its back. It moves itself forward by pushing into the sand with its pushing legs. It plows through the sand like some strange, mechanical toy, churning up small sea creatures as it goes. The sea creatures, mostly worms and crustaceans, are ground up by spines at the bases of its legs. Then the food particles are passed on to its mouth, which is under its large shell, between its legs. It must keep moving in order to eat.

Like the true crabs, horseshoe crabs shed their shells as they grow. True crabs, as you know, back out of their shells. But a horseshoe crab pulls itself out of the front of its shell, which splits across the front and sides. Full-grown females are about twenty inches long. The males are somewhat smaller. These animals are true Easterners. They live all along the Atlantic Coast but never on the Pacific.

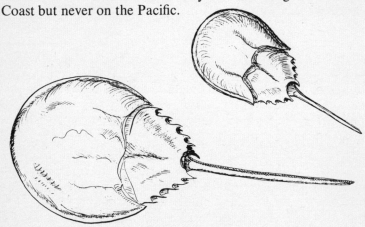

Horseshoe crabs

LOBSTERS. You are more likely to meet a lobster in a sea-food store or on the table than at the seashore. This is because lobsters do not make their homes in tide pools or in the area between low and high tide where you find so many other sea creatures. Lobsters live among the rocks below the low-tide level. They are scavengers, feeding on everything from dead fish to living seaweed. Lobsters are green when they are alive. They turn red only after they have been cooked. Lobsters are not very good swimmers, but they can move swiftly backward by flipping their broad tail fins, which open and shut like a fan.

American Lobsters, which many people call the true lobsters, are found on the Atlantic Coast. They have two large pincer claws. One claw has sharp, pointed teeth for catching and holding food; and the other has rounded teeth for crushing food. The large pincer claws contain delicious lobster meat.

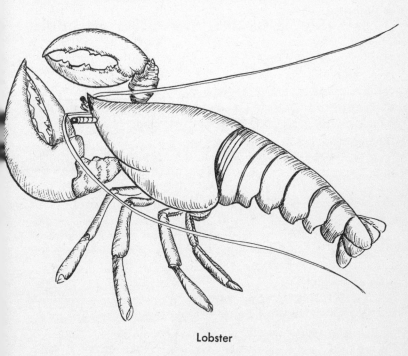

Lobster

Spiny Lobsters, which are found in the Pacific and in southern waters, are distant relatives of the American lobsters. They are often called sea crayfish. Like the American lobster, the spiny lobster is a favorite sea food. It has no pincer claws, however, and hence no juicy claw meat. It has a rough shell that is covered with sharp spines, from which it gets its name.

SHRIMPS. Shrimps are related to crabs and lobsters. All have five pairs of jointed legs and a single solid shell covering head and back. Like lobsters, shrimps swim backward by moving their fanlike tails. Large swimming shrimps are called prawns. When you order "prawns" from a sea-food menu, you know that you will get very large shrimps, usually fried. Other kinds of shrimps, including some that are less than an inch long, are eaten in salads, chowders, and sea-food cocktails. The kinds of shrimps, however, that you are likely to find as you explore the seashore are the very tiny ones that live in sand and tide pools.

Sand Shrimps are the small creatures that you can feel scampering across your bare feet as you walk along the very edge of the water. Waves bring in bits of plant and animal materials and deposit them on the beach. The sand shrimps, which are wonderful scavengers, scurry along the edges of the waves, gathering food and incidentally cleaning up the rubbish. Sand shrimps, which are the color of sand, grow to be two inches long.

Broken-Back Shrimps live in tide pools. They get their name from the way they suddenly bend their backs as they flip their tails to dart backward. They are hard to see, but if you bend over a tide pool for a long time, you may discover one or two of these beautiful little shrimps. If you can catch one, put it in a glassful of sea water long enough to examine its translucent body through your hand lens. You should be able to see its beating heart. After you have studied the shrimp, return it to its tide-pool home.

SAND HOPPERS. Sand hoppers are harmless crustaceans that hop around as though they were fleas. In fact, they are sometimes called sand fleas. Wherever you find piles of rotting seaweed tossed up on the beach, you can watch or catch some sand hoppers. They feed on decaying seaweed and make themselves at home in the shelter of its damp, tangled masses.

Turn over a large clump of old seaweed and you will see dozens of sand hoppers leaping out of the seaweed. They can jump far and high. They use their last three pairs of legs and their tails to help them spring into the air.

BARNACLES. Most crustaceans move about in unusual ways. Some scoot sideways, some hop, some swim forward, and some dart backward through the water. Barnacles, however, do not move about at all, at least not after they have become adults. At the end of the free-swimming larva stage, barnacles attach themselves to rocks, pilings, driftwood, the backs of other crustaceans, the shells of mollusks, and to the bottoms of boats. Once fastened down, the animal grows a protective shell around its body and rests head down for the rest of its life. It can open its shell enough to allow its feathery feet to extend out into the water and brush tiny bits of food into its mouth. When it closes its shell, it can seal in enough water to keep it alive for a long time.

As a barnacle grows, it must cast off its old, tight skin as all crustaceans do. But the skin that molts is inside the protective outer shell. The outside shell grows larger by adding limy material to its edges. If you explore quiet waters where there are many barnacles, you are sure to find some of the molts that have been discarded by the living animals.

Acorn Barnacles are so common along all of our coasts that you cannot miss them. They look like acorns or like little volcanoes. They live fastened to rocks and to the shells of mollusks, attached to wharf pilings, and clustered on ship bottoms. In fact, hulls of ships have to be treated to keep off barnacles and other growths that would cause a drag. There are millions and millions of barnacles along the rocky shores. Watch some of them through the water of a shallow tide pool. Use your hand lens. If you are lucky, you may see them combing the water with their feathery feet in search of food. Perhaps you can find a small rock or a piece of driftwood that is covered with barnacles. If so, place it in a glass bowl filled with cool sea water. Press the bowl into the sand at the edge of the water where the waves and wet sand will keep the bowl cool. Watch the barnacles through your magnifying glass. You should be able to see the animals open and close their shells, extend and draw in their feet, and use them for feeding.

Gooseneck Barnacles are commonly found along the Pacific Coast or far out to sea anchored on pieces of driftwood, empty bottles, or on ships' bottoms. The stalk or gooseneck of this barnacle is fastened by its own cement to some solid or floating surface. Except for its rubbery stalk, this barnacle is much like the acorn barnacle, with a shell that opens and closes as the feathery legs rake in the food.

Now we come to some fresh-water crustaceans. Thus far, all of the crustaceans described in this chapter have been those that live in the sea. Most crustaceans are marine animals. But you will remember reading in Chapter Five about some of the tiny crustaceans that live in fresh water. Daphnia, cyclops, and fairy shrimps are some that you may have found in your miniature aquarium. There are also the gray, green, or brown SCUDS, which are a half-inch to an inch long. They have twelve or more pairs of legs, which they use for grasping, climbing, or swimming. They usually swim on their sides, by waving their legs in the water.

WATER SOW BUGS are also little crustaceans that you may find in fresh water. They live on the bottom of ponds. They are only a half-inch long. They have seven pairs of legs, which they use for crawling around as they eat dead plant material. Neither scuds nor sow bugs are very attractive animals.

CRAYFISH, however, look like little lobsters and are fascinating to watch. They are relatives of the lobsters of the sea and have many of the lobsters' features and habits. A crayfish has five pairs of legs. Its front legs end in strong claws, which are used for catching and holding the small fish, insects, and plant materials on which it feeds. Its jointed tail section ends in a set of fan-shaped swimmerets. The female uses its swimmerets as a brood pouch for eggs, which are fastened on with a kind of glue as they are laid. When the baby crayfish hatch, they cling to the swimmerets, which then serve as a kind of cradle.

Crayfish are easy to discover and easy to catch. Use your tin-can scoop or your bare hands. Since the crayfish is only three to five inches long, you can hold it by its back without getting nipped by its pincer claws. And even if you should get nipped, you would hardly feel it. Look for crayfish along the edge of a pond or stream. You will find them hiding under rocks or peeking out of little tunnels that they make in the

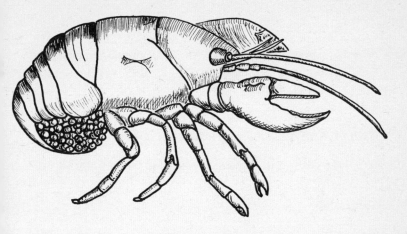

Crayfish carrying eggs

soft mud banks. They feed mainly at night. In the daytime they usually stay at the entrance of their hiding places, their long feelers sticking out to pick up any signs of danger.

When you catch a crayfish, put it in a glass container of cool water from the pond or stream. Add a few stones for the animal to hide under. Offer it some raw meat and watch the way it eats. It will hold the meat in its claws while the mandibles (its chewing jaws) will crush it to pieces. If there are any pieces too tough or too coarse to be swallowed, the crayfish will spit them out.

Notice the way the animal moves. It can both walk and swim, but it swims only when shocked or startled. Then it darts swiftly backward. In walking, the crayfish can move in any direction but usually walks forward, with most of its weight carried by its fourth pair of legs. Turn the crayfish over on its back. You will find that it will have some trouble in turning right side up. It may first roll over on its side, or it may flip itself over by using the muscles in its tail section.

Probably the most useful sense a crayfish has is its sense of touch, which helps it to locate food and to avoid dangers.

Its eyes can help it to locate moving objects and that is about all. Scientists report that there is no evidence that crayfish can hear. When a crayfish seems to be reacting to a sound, it is probably reacting to something it feels with its sense of touch.

Test the senses of a crayfish with some simple experiments. Try attracting it with foods that have different tastes and smells — a bit of fish, a peeled clove of garlic, some celery, and some raw hamburger. Touch it with a soft brush, with your fingers, and with a small stick. Shine a flashlight on it at night. Try to discover which of the crayfish's senses is the most keen.

Scientists tell us that crayfish can form habits and change them. As you observe and experiment with your crayfish, you will be getting acquainted with the behavior of a typical little crustacean.

TWELVE

Frogs and Other Amphibians

Millions and millions of years ago, there were more amphibians on the earth than there are today. It is likely that they were the first animals with backbones to live on land. Their ancestors were fish with fins that were enough like legs to carry them up out of water, and with breathing equipment that made it possible for them to get oxygen from the air. But even though amphibians developed ways of living and breathing out of water, they have not yet lost all of their water-life habits. Perhaps in several million years more, they will be completely adjusted to living on land. But today amphibians still divide their lives between the water world and the world of land and air.

The Latin word *amphibia* means "double life." A typical amphibian lives its first "life" in water and the other "life" on land. Actually, the two "lives" are merely two stages in a single, continuous, and rather unusual life. All amphibians begin as gill-breathing water creatures. Most of them, like the frogs and toads, breathe with lungs and live on land when they are adults. Of course frogs and many other adult amphibians move in and out of water, but they have to breathe air.

In past ages, scientists tell us there were at least five groups of amphibians on the earth. Now there are three main groups left. The first group are wormlike amphibians that live in tropical lands. The second group are the amphibians with tails. Salamanders and newts belong to this group. The third group are the tailless ones, the frogs and toads. There is an old joke that says that a frog's eyes will fall out if you hold it up by its tail. This is impossible to do because no one has ever found a frog with a tail!

There are large numbers of amphibians in the United States. They are interesting animals to study because they have some unusual abilities and habits. Many of them, like the leopard frog, can change their color. Their skin has different pigments — brown, black, and yellow or red. Changes in amount of light and heat cause color changes. When a leopard frog is in bright light or in a very warm place, its skin becomes lighter in color. It turns darker when it is cold or when there is less light. Many frogs and some other amphibians can change skin color.

Amphibians, especially when they are young, have some powers of regeneration. If a leg or a tail is broken off, they can grow new ones. Another of their special abilities is to live all through the winter without food and with very little oxygen. They hibernate in the winter, sleeping in mud at the bottom of ponds. During this time, they take no air into their lungs. The only breathing they do is through their skins. The only nourishment they have is what is stored up in their own bodies. Their temperatures get very low, as cold as the mud that surrounds them. They cannot live, however, if they become completely frozen. Their hearts beat very, very slowly during hibernation. But their hearts *must* beat, and if their hearts freeze, they die. Most amphibians sleep their cold, cold sleep all winter long. Then, when spring comes, the mud they are in grows warmer and the animals rouse themselves and set about getting food, finding mates, and laying eggs, thus starting a whole new generation.

All of the common frogs begin life as eggs. The eggs hatch into tadpoles. The tadpoles grow into adults. As adults, they have skin that is moist, smooth, and rather slippery. They have long, long tongues that are fastened to the front of their mouths. These tongues can be flicked out as fast as lightning to catch an insect or a water creature. Frogs eat flies, mosquitoes, and other insects, many of which are harmful to man. They also eat worms, fish, tadpoles, and other frogs. A frog has such a large mouth that it can swallow a creature almost as big as itself. When a frog goes into the water, a transparent, watertight covering rolls over its eyes. The top half of this eye-covering helps it to look up and see above the water. The bottom half makes it easy for it to look down into the water.

Frogs make interesting sounds. You have probably heard the chirping, musical voices of spring peepers on a summer evening and the deep croaking sounds of bullfrogs. These frog songs are made by the males at mating time. Frogs sing with their mouths shut. Air is taken in through nostrils and passed over vocal cords on the way to the lungs. As a frog sings, a balloon-like vocal sac swells out at its throat. This sac acts as a sound amplifier, helping the small animal to make sounds that are very loud for its size.

Frogs and toads must keep their skins somewhat moist. When they are very young, this is especially important. After a summer rain you may see many tiny toads and frogs hopping around in puddles on sidewalks and roads. As they grow, frogs and toads shed their skin. When this happens, they use their front feet like hands to peel off the old skin. Then, unless they shed their skin in water, they stuff the skin into their mouths and swallow it, all very neatly.

The three most common kinds of tailless amphibians found in the United States and Canada are frogs, toads, and tree "toads," which are really small tree-climbing frogs. Hyla is a kind of tree frog you may discover climbing around on tree limbs and twigs, clinging to bark, or hanging on to reeds at the water's edge. This little frog has sticky disks at the ends of its fingers and toes. The disks or suckers make it easy for hyla frogs to climb.

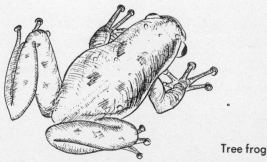

Tree frog

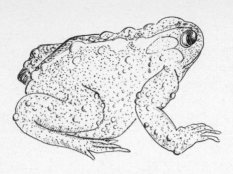

Garden toad

Toads are like frogs except for the skin. A frog's skin is smooth and somewhat slimy. But the skin of a toad feels drier and is covered with warty bumps. These bumps are not warts but are really glands. The glands produce a liquid that is annoying or poisonous to the toad's enemies. It cannot hurt you to handle a toad. The liquid from its "warts" will not cause warts or anything else on your skin. However, if you should *swallow* any of the liquid, you would probably become very sick indeed. So — look at a toad, hold it, stroke it with your fingers, and make a pet of it if you wish, but try never to swallow it!

The tongue of a toad is like that of a frog. Because of their handy, sticky-tipped tongues, toads are able to catch and eat enormous quantities of insects and other small creatures. Beetles, cutworms, flies, caterpillars, slugs, snails, sow bugs, and other creeping and crawling and flying creatures are food for toads. Scientists have figured out that a single toad can eat about ten thousand insects in a three-month period. It is no wonder we welcome toads when they find their way to our gardens!

If you can find a toad to observe, notice the two very large "warts" (glands) just back of the eyes. Notice, too, how the toad's skin color blends with the color of the soil, leaves, and bark. Watch the way the toad seems to drop off to sleep until — *zip!* — out flashes its deadly tongue to catch some little

Tongue of frog or toad

creature that has carelessly come too close. The tidbit is flipped into the toad's mouth and swallowed. Then the tongue is re-coiled in the front of its mouth, ready to be shot out again the moment another tempting bite comes within striking distance.

Since all toads, as well as frogs, like and need moisture, your garden toad will enjoy summer showers. Make a shower with a sprinkling can or hose. Water in your garden will make it an attractive place for amphibians.

If you live in Southern California, Nevada, Utah, Arizona, New Mexico, Texas, or on the dry western plains, you will find few, if any, frogs or toads. These areas do not provide enough moist meadows, swampy fields, or other damp hunting grounds. But in most other places in the United States and Canada (except in very cold climates) you can find frogs and toads within hopping distance of any body of fresh water. (They do not live in salt water nor in salty swamps and marshes.)

How long does it take for a tadpole to change into a frog or toad? You may have asked this question or just wondered about it. Now you can find the answer, or at least part of the answer, by doing some scientific exploring. First of all, you will need to visit a pond or a slow-moving stream. A pond in a city park, a stream by a golf course, a little pool in the woods, or a small slow river that wanders through the mead-ows — these are the kinds of places where you are likely to find tadpoles. You may call them polliwogs, but tadpoles is their proper name.

Kneel by the edge of the water and look for fat little tadpoles wiggling around among the water weeds. If it is spring or very early summer, the tadpoles will be very small and you may find some of the eggs from which the tadpoles have not yet hatched. These eggs have been laid in a jelly-like mass by the mother frog or toad. If you can reach some of the eggs, scoop them up with your kitchen-strainer scoop and dump them into a glass jar of pond water. Then look at the eggs carefully. Even without your hand lens, you can see a tiny, unhatched tadpole inside each transparent egg. If you are very lucky, you may see a baby tadpole wriggle out of its egg. As soon as you have examined the eggs, put them back into the water and watch the eggs and tadpoles in their natural home.

Each little tadpole has to look after itself from the very beginning. There are no parents around to take care of these babies. They must find their own plant material to eat. They must take in water through their round little mouths and let it pass through their gills, where oxygen goes right into the blood stream. Then the water must pass out through tiny gill holes, one on the left side of each tadpole's head. Each little tadpole must swim and keep away from its enemies. Otherwise, it will be eaten by bigger tadpoles, grown-up frogs, fish, turtles, water bugs, or almost anything in the water that is larger than itself. As you peer into the shallow water, you can watch some of the life-and-death struggle that goes on as a baby tadpole begins its free-swimming days.

In order to observe tadpoles more closely and to make some scientific records, you need to collect some of the eggs or some of the newly hatched tadpoles. Have ready the following materials for "operation tadpole":

    a kitchen-strainer scoop for catching tadpoles and eggs
    several plastic cans
    plastic covers (with air holes punched in them) to fit the cans
    a box or basket in which to carry home the filled cans
    a large clean pail or can
    a bowl or wide-mouthed glass jar to be used as a tadpole aquarium

All the items except the last one make up your field equipment. They should be taken with you on your tadpole hunt. Plastic cans (the kind in which ice cream is sold) are ideal. They are light in weight and will not break if dropped. Clean tin cans, especially coffee cans, are next best. If you use these, punch holes in the covers. The covers will keep the water from sloshing out, while the holes will let in enough air to keep your specimens alive until you get them home.

Take your field equipment to the edge of the pond or stream where you first observed the tadpoles and eggs. Fill the plastic or tin cans with water. Then, with your scoop, gather up some of the jelly-like eggs and a few of the tiniest tadpoles you can find. Since the eggs usually hatch out in spring and early summer, you may be able to find only eggs if you are collecting early in the season, or only tadpoles if you are collecting in midsummer or later. But if it is early in the summer, you should find both eggs and tadpoles. Put the eggs, or the tadpoles, or both eggs and tadpoles into the plastic or tin cans you have ready. Do not put more than about a dozen (eggs and tadpoles) into a single can. Once the eggs and tadpoles have been placed in cans, put on the covers, and do not let the cans stand where they can get warm. One way to keep them cool is to stand them right in the water. Make a little underwater nest of stones for each can. Put the can down into it, with a heavy stone across the top. Fresh water can run in and out of the holes in the can if you are careful not to put the stone over all of the holes.

After you have caught your living specimens, fill your pail or large can with water. Add bits of green pond scum, which will continue to grow in your aquarium and will serve as food for the young tadpoles. If you can find some very small floating water plants, add these, too. You will need to carry home enough water from the pond or stream to fill your aquarium. If possible, take home more than enough water. Then, as the aquarium water evaporates, you can keep adding the same kind of water without having to make extra trips.

When you have finished your collecting, pack your specimen cans in a box or basket and cover them with wet weeds to keep them cool on the way home. The tadpoles and the eggs may die if they get too warm. They should be kept about as cool as they were in their natural environment.

As soon as you get home, fill the bowl or jar you are going to use for an aquarium. Pour in the pond or stream water and add the algae and water plants. Then add the tadpoles or the eggs or both. Keep the aquarium in a cool place, perhaps outdoors on a porch or patio, or in a window. It should get the sun for an hour or two each day, but the water should never be allowed to get really warm. The amount of sun you give it will depend on where you live. If you live in a very hot climate, your aquarium will need protection from the sun most of the day. In a cooler climate, it can stand more sun. You will have to watch carefully for the first few days. Try to provide enough sun for the plants, including the green algae, to grow, and yet not enough sun for the water to become warm and soupy. If the egg mass turns cloudy and white, you will know that the eggs are not developing. If this happens, all you can do is to take out any live tadpoles you may have, empty the aquarium, wash it well with clear water, and start over again.

In most cases, the eggs will continue to develop in their new home. Soon they will hatch, perhaps right before your eyes. Watch the hatching process through your hand lens. Write down the date of the first hatching. It is only a few days to a few weeks from the time of laying that the eggs of frogs and toads hatch into tadpoles.

The feeding of tadpoles is not difficult. Try feeding different things to your young specimens. Make a note of the things they seem to prefer. Here is a list of things some tadpoles like to eat:

algae from the pond, or the algae that grow on plant leaves and on the walls of the aquarium

tiny pieces of raw lettuce

tiny pieces of cooked or raw spinach

bits of the yolk of a hard-boiled egg

tiny bits of raw liver or raw beef (for the tadpoles as they get bigger)

Now, as you watch your tadpoles develop, keep a daily record of what they are doing. In this way, you will discover the life history of a group of interesting little creatures. Watch for the stages listed below. They are typical for all tadpoles.

For the first few days after hatching out, the tiny tadpoles hold on to the bottom of the aquarium or to plant stems or leaves by means of little suckers that are located on their undersides. Their mouths are not yet open. They have outside gills on each side of their heads.

After a few days, their mouths open and they begin to swim around. The gills become covered by folds of skin. A breathing hole is left open on the left side of each tadpole's head. The water is taken in through the mouth, passed through the gills and out through the breathing hole.

Some time during its first or second summer (depending upon the kind of toad or frog that is developing) the tadpole begins to turn into an adult. When this stage is reached, there are bulges on the tadpole's body, one on each side, about where the tail joins the body. Gradually these bulges become the hind legs.

Next, little bulges begin to swell out near the head. One day one of these bulges turns into the left front leg, which pushes out through the breathing hole. Soon after, the right front leg breaks right through the skin. Since the breathing hole is now closed by the front leg, the tadpole has to keep its mouth open most of the time, letting water in and out through the mouth.

About this time, the tadpole climbs out of the water and begins to breathe air. Its gills have been replaced by lungs for air breathing. Using its four new legs, the tadpole pulls itself up on a rock or a board or whatever it finds that will get it out of the water.

Now a most interesting thing happens. The tadpole actually absorbs its own tail! As it sits there out of the water, it does not need any food because it gets enough body nourishment from its tail. Its tail gets shorter and shorter. And then one day, there is no tail at all! This marks the end of the tadpole. It has changed to a frog or a toad. When this happens, take it to a moist, green place beside the pond or stream where you collected the eggs and caught the tadpoles. Frogs and toads need to hop and to swim, to eat insects and small water creatures, and to have freedom, which you cannot provide in an aquarium or cage.

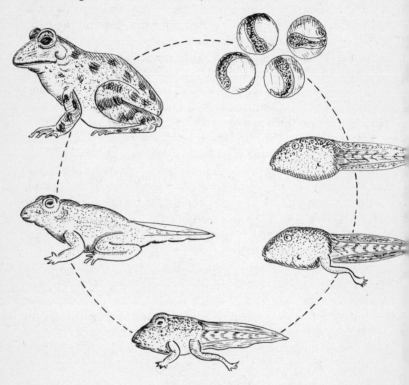

Life cycle of a frog

As you observe your tadpoles passing through these various stages, write down the date when each stage is reached by the first tadpole, and the date when the last of your specimens reaches it. Notice how long it takes for the average of your tadpoles to reach each of the stages. You might also like to keep a chart or a notebook of these stages, with drawings from life of each stage. You could keep the dates on such a record, too.

Now, return to your original question: "How long does it take for a tadpole to become a frog or toad?" Count the number of days between the date of hatching and the date when most of the specimens became four-legged, tailless air-breathers. Your experiment may have demonstrated some tadpoles changing to little frogs over a period of two months. An unscientific thinker might decide that such an experiment proves that it takes two months for all tadpoles to develop into frogs. Of course, it proves nothing of the sort! It merely shows that a particular group of tadpoles, under certain conditions, developed into frogs in two months. A scientific person would write his conclusions in about those words.

But here are some interesting facts. For tadpoles to reach adulthood may take a few weeks, or all summer, or a whole year, or even two years! Why are there so many possibilities?

To answer this question, you may have to do some reading about toads and frogs. If you do, you will find that little spring peepers develop in a couple of weeks, toads and some frogs require a longer time, and the big bullfrogs do not develop until after one or two years in the tadpole stage.

We usually think of tadpoles as frogs and toads in the baby stage. Actually, salamanders and other amphibians with tails also develop from tadpoles. In the case of salamanders, however, the babies are usually called larvae rather than tadpoles. The larva of a salamander can be recognized by its fringe of gills, which look like frilly wings on the sides of its head. When a salamander becomes an air-breathing land animal, the gill fringe disappears.

People sometimes confuse salamanders with lizards because both animals have much the same shape, size, and quick, darting movements. Lizards, however, are reptiles, which always have scales of some sort. Salamanders, like other amphibians, have smooth skin with no hint of scales. They feed on living food, eating the same kinds of creatures as frogs and toads.

One of the most attractive as well as most common of the American salamanders is the newt. The spotted newt (greenish-brown or olive green, with dots of black, rcd, and yellow) can be found in ponds and quiet streams. They are slow-moving animals. You can pick them up with your fingers. Newts can be kept in a terrarium, which you can make in a wire cage or a box or an old aquarium. (If the aquarium is cracked, it will not matter for this purpose.) Put gravel and damp soil on the bottom of the terrarium. Plant it with moss, grass, and other tiny plants. Make a swimming pool in a glass or enamel dish and put in into the terrarium. Surround the little pool with rocks and natural foliage. The pool should be deep enough and wide enough for the salamander to swim in.

Many newts pass through an interesting stage, one not common to other amphibians. After they have been larvae (tadpoles) all summer, they grow legs, lose their gills and tail fin, and change into slim little red creatures called efts. Efts live on land for a year or two and then return to the water and change into adult salamanders. If you can find some of these attractive red efts, capture two or three of them for your terrarium. Efts are only about two inches long. Adult newts are a little over three inches. They are easy to care for in a terrarium. They can be trained to eat raw meat from the end of a tooth pick or broom straw, or even from your fingers. During the winter newts become sluggish and sleepy. Then they need less food. But by spring they are again active, hungry, and alert.

THIRTEEN

Reptiles in and on the Water

The very word *reptile* fills some people with dread. For some reason, human beings and reptiles seem to be afraid of each other. You may be afraid of snakes. Snakes are probably even more afraid of you. Too often we think of reptiles as being sneaky, slithering creatures lying in wait and ever ready to strike out with a deadly fang or a mouthful of sharp teeth. Actually, nearly all reptiles are extremely timid, easily frightened, and wanting only to run away from their enemies and hide.

Today there are only four main groups of reptiles: snakes, lizards, turtles, and the crocodiles and alligators. There is also a rare kind of reptile, the tuatara, which is found only in New Zealand. The tuatara looks like the dinosaurs of millions of years ago when many kinds of reptiles roamed the earth. Then, in what is often referred to as the Age of Reptiles, these strange-looking creatures were completely at home. Some were small and some were gigantic. They all laid eggs, from which the young hatched into tiny creatures that looked just like their parents. They breathed air through lungs and had dry skins that were made of scales or plates. Most of today's reptiles have the same characteristics as their dinosaur ancestors of the long-ago past. As you observe the reptiles that live near your ponds and streams, think of them as the direct descendants of the animals of the Reptile Age. They seem odd, strange, and often awkward in appearance and behavior. Perhaps they are just very, very old-fashioned — about seventy million years out of date!

It is true that some reptiles can be dangerous to man. There are so few of these in the United States, however, that they can be listed below.

Dangerous Lizard: only one kind, the Gila monster, found only in the hot desert country of Mexico and in the southwest United States

Dangerous Snakes: the rattlesnake, found in most parts of the United States; pit vipers (the copperhead and the cottonmouth or water moccasin), found in eastern and southern United States; and the coral snake, found in southern United States

Dangerous Turtle: only one type, the snapping turtle, found in eastern, central, and southern United States

Dangerous Crocodile: only the large American crocodile, found in southern Florida. (American alligators are not usually dangerous.)

Other kinds of reptiles are not harmful to man. In fact, most of them are helpful, since they keep down the population of insects, rats, mice, gophers, and other pests. They are also interesting since they, like the amphibians, show so clearly their relationship to their prehistoric ancestors.

Amphibians, as you know, are still dependent upon the water world for at least part of their lives. Reptiles, however, are not really water creatures, even though some of them live in and on the water. They all must breathe air all of their lives. They have no gills at any stage of development. As you discover turtles, water snakes, and perhaps even alligators and crocodiles at the water's edge, remember that there are many, many reptiles that do not live near water at all. The so-called horned toad of the western desert, for instance, probably never sees any body of water in its whole life. If it were really a toad, this could not be true, for toads must begin life as water-living tadpoles. But the horny creature is not a toad. It is a true lizard, and like all lizards is an air breather all of its life.

Lizards are the most numerous of all the reptile family. You can find them in woods, fields, gardens, and deserts, scampering over the ground, blinking in the sun, sipping drops of water from a faucet, or hiding timidly under rocks. You may find some lizards in or near the water, but the most common lizards are land animals.

There are some common snakes, however, that live by and in fresh water. Water snakes, which are found mainly in the eastern United States, are dark reddish brown, or olive green, or marked with tan and black barred or diamond patterns. They are fairly large snakes, three to five feet long. They swim rapidly under water and on the surface. Unlike most other snakes, which lay eggs, water snakes have live babies. They have dozens of them at a time, tiny, wriggling snakes that look just like their parents. Water snakes are not poisonous. However, unless you are an *expert* at recognizing snakes, do not try to catch a water snake. It is possible to mistake a dangerous diamond-marked rattler or a dark brown cottonmouth for a harmless water snake. If you are especially interested in snakes, learn about them in zoos, museums, and in field books before you attempt to catch any. You might make a mistake that could cause you sickness or even death — if you handled a poisonous snake. It is even more likely that any snake you caught would experience sickness and death. Snakes often refuse to eat while in captivity.

Turtles, however, are quite different in this and in other respects. All except the snapping turtles can be caught, handled, examined, fed, and even kept as pets. A turtle is a true reptile, with all of the family characteristics. Its skin has scales or plates, it lays eggs, it breathes air through its lungs, and it has been on the earth for a very long time. In fact, turtles have been on the earth for about two hundred million years and have changed very little in all that time! There is one branch of the turtle family that lives on land. Land turtles are called tortoises. They have high boxlike shells and club-shaped feet. Other turtles are water creatures with webbed feet or flippers for swimming.

Sea turtles are often huge animals more than a ton in weight. They have flippers, which are fine for swimming but not very good for walking around. This is no handicap for the sea turtle because it spends most of its life in the sea. At egg-laying time the female drags its cumbersome body up the beach to lay about one hundred and fifty eggs in a hollow place in the sand above the high-tide level. The heat of the sun helps the eggs to hatch. After about two months, the baby turtles crawl out of the eggs. They then find their way down to the edge of the water, where, with the help of a wave or two to carry them to deep water, they take up their lives in the sea.

Other turtles live in lakes and ponds, where they eat insects, worms, fish, and some plant materials. They have no teeth. Their hard, horny beaks, which often have sharp edges, are used for tearing up food. They can also be used to give you a painful nip or pinch if the turtles are annoyed.

A turtle has a most unusual skeleton. It is a vertebrate (animal with a backbone), but its backbone and ribs are grown into the upper part of its shell. In fact, the upper shell, called a carapace, is formed from overgrown, widened ribs. The bottom part of the shell is called the plastron. Between the carapace and the plastron are the turtle's flesh and vital organs. The hard, bony shells protect its soft parts. In time of danger, most turtles can draw themselves into their shells for protection. Snapping turtles, however, have small shells. The plastron is especially small, leaving the animal's legs, long neck and head, and much of its underside unprotected by shell. To defend itself, this kind of turtle snaps at and bites its enemies. Other turtles usually just draw themselves into their heavy shells when frightened.

Like all reptiles, turtles are cold-blooded. This does not mean that their blood is always cold. Cold-blooded animals take their temperature from their surroundings. In cold water, their blood is cold. In the hot sun, their blood warms up. With warm-blooded animals, the blood temperature remains about the same regardless of how hot or cold it is outside the body. Cold-blooded animals are very dependent on their surroundings. They must find shade when the sun is very hot, and a warm place when there is a sharp chill in the air. Otherwise, they could become sick and die from extreme changes in the temperature of their blood. Since water does not change temperature nearly as quickly as air does, cold-blooded creatures, like turtles, can easily keep comfortable and healthy in the water.

Turtles do much of their feeding in the water. They eat tadpoles, worms, insects, fish, and some plant materials. They lay their eggs on land, usually in a hole in soft earth. The mother turtle covers the eggs with twigs, leaves, or soil and then goes off, leaving the eggs to be hatched by the sun's warmth. Snakes and skunks and other animals may eat the eggs before they hatch. Crows and other birds and animals may eat the soft-shelled babies after they have hatched. The parents do nothing to protect their eggs or their young. The baby turtles that manage to avoid being caught and eaten by their enemies find their way to water, where they feed on small water life. If a turtle survives its danger-filled and unprotected babyhood, it has a chance to live for a long, long time. In fact, turtles have been known to live longer than any other vertebrate animal. Probably sixty years is a good average life span for a turtle, but some have been known to live for more than a hundred and fifty years. Man (or rather *woman*) is the longest-living mammal. But it has never been proved that a human being has ever lived to be as old as some of the oldest turtles.

Turtles seem to be deaf. But their other senses, sight, smell, and taste, are well developed. They are fairly intelligent, can be trained, and many of them make amusing pets. If you want a turtle to raise, don't buy one that has pictures or "Souvenir of Los Angeles" or anything else painted on its shell. The paint will injure the shell and may make the turtle sick. If someone gives you a turtle that has been painted, remove the paint by wiping with a few drops of nail-polish remover and then wash the shell in cold water. It is easy to catch a baby turtle in a lake or pond by using your long-handled strainer scoop. You can make a good home for a small turtle or two by using a large fish bowl. Build an island of stones in the center to give the turtles a place to climb out of the water.

You can also make an attractive turtle home in a wire cage or a terrarium. Here are some things to put into it:

Soil, green grass, and other small plants to provide a fresh natural-looking area where turtles can wander around when they climb out of the water

Stones and pieces of wood under which the turtles can hide

A shallow bowl (glass or china) filled with water and edged with stones

A cloth or magazine across part of the cage to provide some shade during the hottest part of the day

A few pennies in the water to provide copper, which keeps the turtles' shells from getting soft

Turtle home in a fish bowl

Turtles are not hard to feed. They like live food (worms, moths, slugs, insects, small snails), but will also eat bits of lean hamburger and other raw meat. Bits of lettuce, and some bone meal or powdered egg shells, will help keep your turtles strong. Place the food in the water or on a stone at the water's edge. Most of the turtle food sold in stores is made of ant eggs and dried insects. The turtles may eat this dried food, but they will be much healthier if you feed them fresh food. If you bring a bit of raw meat to your turtles each day, they will quickly learn to take it from the tips of your fingers. They will even learn to come to the side of the cage near you as soon as they see you standing there. Perhaps they can recognize you. Or perhaps they just smell the fresh meat you are bringing.

Since turtles are air breathers, you can safely hold one in your hand, play with it on the grass, and watch its peculiar dragging pace as it moves along. Get acquainted with a turtle and then use your magnifying glass to study it closely.

Notice the separate scales or plates that form the pattern on its back. On many kinds of turtles, a new edge is added to each plate every summer. By counting the number of rims, or rings, on a single plate, you can tell the age of the turtle. When it hatches, a turtle has fairly smooth plates, each with a single edge. After a year, there will be an inner ridge on each plate. After two years, two inner ridges, and so on, as long as the turtle keeps growing. However, on the shell of a very old turtle, the plates may be quite smooth because the growth ridges have worn away with age. Look at your small turtles and find out how many summers they have lived.

Growth rings on plates of turtle shell

As you examine the shell, you will notice that the carapace is rounded while the plastron on the underside is rather flat. Look for the two bridges that connect the plastron and the carapace. The bridges keep the top and bottom shells apart as well as help to hold the turtle's body safely inside. If you look at a number of turtles, you may discover that on some the plastron is slightly bent inward. These are the males. On the females, the plastrons curve outward. The males have the longer tails but are usually smaller otherwise than the females. Both males and females have claws on their feet, which they use for holding their food and tearing it apart.

If you should ever find the empty shell of a dead turtle, look at the inside. You will see clearly where the ribs and backbone have grown together to form the inner part of the carapace. If you should find a turtle that has died recently and is still in its shell, you can remove the soft parts by boiling the whole thing and then picking out the flesh. You can learn quite a bit about turtles by examining a well-preserved shell. The turtle's shell is an effective kind of armor. This is probably one reason why turtles have lasted so long on this earth.

Since turtles have no way of regulating their body temperature, they must always be able to crawl into a little cave or other shady nook in the heat of the day. They need some sunshine, but too much sun can cause death to a turtle. In cold weather, your turtles will probably hibernate. They will draw into their shells and seem to be asleep. During the cold months they will eat very little. But when spring comes, they will become active and hungry once more.

There are about two hundred and fifty different kinds of turtles alive today. Below are listed a few of the common kinds that you may be able to find in lakes, ponds, and slow streams.

Mud turtles like to sun themselves in shallow water but seldom climb on shore. They are about four inches long and have wide plastrons that are hinged so that they can be pulled inward to give extra protection when head and limbs are drawn under the shell. They are usually all one color (brown) with no special markings. They have a strong odor, but not so strong as the turtles described next.

Musk turtles are named for their strong musky odor, which is probably a defense against enemies. They are much like mud turtles except for the plastron, which is narrower on the musk turtle.

Snapping turtles are to be avoided. They have very long necks and powerful jaws. A large one could bite off a finger.

Snappers live in quiet muddy water, where they feed on fish and other water life. Their plastrons are very small, looking like little bibbed aprons fastened across their middles. Full-grown common snapping turtles grow to be a foot and a half long. One kind of snapping turtle is the largest of all fresh-water turtles. It lies on the muddy bottom, its ugly mouth open, ready to grasp its prey. An adult weighs about a hundred and fifty pounds and has jaws large and strong enough to crush a hand. Snappers can easily be recognized by the sharply pointed plates on their shells and by their unusually fierce-looking mouths, which are tipped by strong, pointed beaks.

Painted turtles are the most common kinds, and the ones you are most likely to find in your exploring trips. They are easily recognized by the attractive red markings on the border of the carapace and on the yellow-striped skin of the head. The plastron is yellow, sometimes edged with red. Full grown, they are five or six inches long. They eat only in the water. Small painted turtles make good pets but are not easy to catch because they are shy and can dive quickly when approached. Once caught and safely in your turtle cage, they will adjust to captivity and will soon learn to eat from your fingers.

Spotted turtles are also very common. These little fellows (three to five inches long) have smooth dark shells dotted with orange or yellow. Like the painted turtles, these make good pets and will thrive in captivity especially if they can eat in water.

There are other kinds of turtles, on land, in the sea, and in fresh water. They form an interesting group of animals. But, like all reptiles, their great age is in the past. They continue to live on the earth, but, except as scientific curiosities, they are not very important in the present world.

FOURTEEN

How to Be a Fish Watcher

As you look down among the water weeds that grow at the edge of a pond, you are sure to see fish: darting little flecks of minnows, or a long brown fish lying like a shadow against the bottom, or a flash of silver as a fish breaks the water in an arched leap. At the seashore, too, you are likely to find fish in the deeper tide pools, and perhaps some that have been stranded in the shallows as the tide went out. Bend over, put your face close to the surface of the water, and watch the fish. To get a really good look, try using a large, clear glass bowl. Push the dish down into the water, as deep as you can without letting the water reach the top. The glass will reduce the glare of the sun on the wavy water.

With or without a glass dish, you can observe fish. Watch the way they use their tails and fins to propel themselves through the water. Notice that they can also hover in one place, almost without any motion. Look at differences in shape, size, color, and in special features. There are so many fish and so many differences among them.

There are known to be twenty-five thousand different species of fish on the earth today. This is almost as many as all the kinds of mammals, birds, reptiles, and amphibians *combined*. Why, you may wonder, are there so very many different kinds of fish? Scientists who specialize in the study of fish (ichthyologists) can explain this great variety.

Nearly three-fifths of the earth's surface is covered with water, and practically all of this water is inhabited by fish. But some of the water is salty and some is fresh; some is pure and clear and some is dank and murky; and there are different kinds and amounts of chemicals dissolved in the waters of the world. There are differences, too, in depth and movement of different bodies of water. There are the deep and drifting waters of mid-ocean; the sunny shallows; the dashing waterfalls and churning rapids; the rolling waves and swelling tides; and the placid surfaces of protected lakes. Some bodies of water are literally ice-cold. Others are cool, tepid, or warm. And a few are too hot for human comfort. Yet, in nearly all of these different kinds of water, fish make their homes. How can they do it? Because, through generations and generations, they have developed different features. They have adjusted to their different kinds of water environments.

Think of all the kinds of fish you have ever seen — in colored photographs, in fish markets, in a tank in a pet store, in a movie or on a television program, in an aquarium, at the end of your fish line, or swimming around in their native homes. There are fish of every color of the rainbow, thick ones and thin ones, toothless ones and ones with jaws lined with fierce teeth. There are snub-nosed fish and some with long beaks. There are fish with feelers and some with winglike fins, some with lights along their sides, some with sharp spines, some with tails like swords and others with hardly any tails at all. Yet, with all the many differences that fish have developed, nearly all of them have five important characteristics in common. As you look at a fish, keep in mind, THIS ANIMAL IS A FISH BECAUSE . . .

> it is cold-blooded, and
> it is completely aquatic, and
> it is a vertebrate, and
> it breathes by means of gills, and
> its heart has two chambers.

Originally (many, many millions of years ago) most fish lived in the seas. Gradually, some fish began coming up the rivers into fresh waters to mate or to lay eggs. Some of them made themselves at home in fresh water and gradually became permanent fresh-water species. Others still move from sea to fresh water and then back again. In addition to the fish that migrated from sea to fresh-water environments, there are kinds that probably developed from the beginning in inland bodies of water or, if they ever came from the sea, it was so long ago that their salt-water history is lost in remote geologic ages.

When you go to the edge of a pond or stream to explore fresh-water fish life, take with you a glass dish to look through, a long-handled cloth net for catching specimens, a pail or a kettle with a handle for carrying them, and your magnifying glass for making careful observations. You may also want to take with you some food with which to lure the fish. Try bread crumbs, small insects, and some commercial dried fish food. Scatter bits of food on the water and watch the fish as they nibble it.

Among the smallest of these fresh-water fish there are some that can be caught and raised in a home aquarium. They can be kept at ordinary room temperature and are not too fussy about their food. Different kinds of minnows, Johnny Darters, and small young catfish, sunfish, and sticklebacks are interesting to catch and raise.

MINNOWS. There are several kinds of minnows, all of them short and slender. They are the tiny silvery fish that are so plentiful in most ponds and streams. Some of them flash with iridescent colors as the sun shines on them.

Minnows are often caught to be used as bait for catching larger fish. A happier fate for a minnow is to be caught by you and placed in an aquarium. You will find that minnows make attractive aquarium fish. Feed them any kind of prepared fish food, small earthworms, insects, and bits of raw meat. Some minnows can be trained to leap out of the water after a bit of raw meat that is dangled over the water on the end of a string.

Minnows, which belong to the same family as carp and goldfish, are in many ways typical of most of the common fish of the world. Observe a minnow swimming around, either in its natural home or in your aquarium. If you do not have a minnow to watch, try to find a goldfish to look at. Look at its five kinds of fins and the way in which each kind is used to help the fish move about.

By moving its tail from side to side, the fish moves itself forward. The caudal fin is on the tail. It moves with the tail and helps to propel the fish forward. It also serves as a kind of rudder for steering. Notice how differently the caudal fins are shaped on different kinds of fish. Most minnows have caudal fins that are V-shaped at the end. Some goldfish have skimpy little caudal fins. Others have tail fins that look like long, trailing feathers.

Look next at the dorsal fins, the ones that stand up like sails along the top edge of a fish's back. The front dorsal is usually stiff and spiny. The rear dorsal is softer. On some fish the front and rear dorsal are combined into a single short fin. On others, there are two separate dorsals across the middle and the rear of the fish's back. Dorsal fins help to keep the fish straight up and down as it moves through the water.

Notice the fin on the underside, just back of the vent. This is called the anal fin. Like the dorsal fin on the top, this bottom fin helps to stabilize the fish's movements.

Watch the way your fish specimen is using the two pairs of fins that grow out from its sides. The pair near the head are called pectoral fins. The other pair, nearer the middle, are the pelvic fins. These four fins correspond to the four legs found on many other kinds of vertebrates. The pectorals and pelvics are important fins for swimming. The fish uses them like paddles or oars for backing up, turning, stopping, and staying in one place.

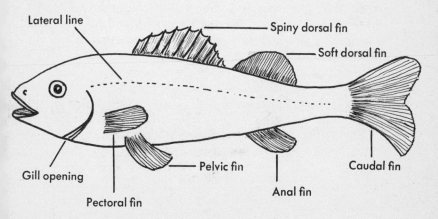

External parts of a fish

You will notice that your fish, with only a slight fluttering wave of its pairs of fins, is able to keep itself in one place. It neither floats to the top nor sinks to the bottom. How is it able to do this, since its body, being made of flesh and skin and bones, is heavier than an equal volume of water? It would sink to the bottom once the swimming motions stopped if it were not for a special air bladder located between its stomach and its backbone. The gas in this balloon-like sac makes it possible for it to remain suspended in water without much exertion.

Watch your fish through your magnifying glass and notice how it keeps opening its mouth to take in water. It does this, not because it is thirsty and taking drinks, but because this is a fish's way of breathing. (The water goes in through the fish's mouth and is then passed through the gills.) If you watch closely, you can see the gill covers move as the fish lets the water out. Gills are special organs that remove oxygen from the air that is dissolved in the water. In passing through the gills, the water flows over *miles* of tiny tubes that carry blood. The oxygen goes right through the thin walls of these tubes and into the fish's bloodstream. The gills also discharge carbon dioxide, which is carried out of the fish's body with the water that is expelled from under the gill covers.

Try this experiment to see how fish breathe in water. Put one small fish into a white bowl filled with some of the water it has been living in. Have ready a bottle of harmless liquid

Gill cover removed to show gills

food coloring. Watch the fish as it opens its mouth to take in water. As it does so, put one drop of food coloring on the water right over the mouth. As soon as some of the colored water is taken into the fish's mouth, watch for it to come out from under the gill covers. It goes in carrying oxygen and it comes out carrying carbon dioxide, but the appearance of the colored water will not be changed.

If you were to watch your fish until it closed its eyes, do you know how long it would take? It would be a long, long watch, because fish have no eyelids. They can never shut their eyes! Our eyelids cover our eyes every few moments in order to keep our eyes bathed in moisture. Since fish are always in moisture, they do not need covers for their eyes. While you are looking at your fish's eyes, notice how large the pupils are. Most fish have pupils that seem big for their bodies. Large pupils can take in large amounts of light. Since fish must do much of their seeing in the semidarkness under water, large pupils are useful. In fact, many kinds of fish have unusually good eyesight. They often depend on sight for their main contact with the rest of the world. Think how accurately a trout will strike at a fisherman's bait.

Fish have other senses, too. They can taste and smell. They have two nose holes, or nostrils, which they use only for smelling, since they do not breathe through their noses. Fish can hear too, but they have their ears hidden on the inside of their heads.

Most fish have a long mark or dent on each side of their bodies. This mark extends from the gill covers to the tail. It is the lateral line canal, with which the fish can sense vibrations in the water.

Minnows, goldfish, and many other kinds of fish are covered with scales. Study the pattern of the scales through your hand lens. You will notice that each scale grows separately from the skin. Scales grow at angles, overlapping each other like shingles on a roof. During the summer each scale grows larger, making a growth ring. There is very little growth during the winter, just enough to show a narrow ridge. Get some fish scales the next time someone scales fish at your house. If you cannot get any scales at home, ask for some at a fish market or butcher shop. Look at the separate scales through your magnifying glass. By counting the growth rings (a wide ring for the summer, a narrow line or ridge for the winter), you should be able to tell the age of the fish that produced each of the scales.

As you look at the fish scales, you will notice their beautiful shine and color. You will also notice that your fingers get very sticky from handling them. The stickiness is from the film of slime that forms a protective coating on a fish's body. If a live fish is handled and some of the slime rubbed off, the fish may die. The slime not only protects the scales and skin, but also makes it easier for the fish to slip through the water.

Most fish lay eggs. The female lays many, many eggs. Most of them are eaten by other creatures or destroyed in one way or another. A few of them manage to survive until the baby fish hatch out. Tiny newly hatched fish, as well as fish eggs, make tasty meals for larger fish. Some minnows and a few other kinds of fish protect their eggs and their young. With some species, the female lays the eggs in a nest that has been made by the male. The male then stands guard and watches over the eggs until they hatch. Some males also watch over the newly hatched fish. Most fish, however, just lay their eggs in the water and leave the rest to chance.

If you keep your minnows or goldfish for a year or more, and if there is plenty of space in your aquarium, the females may lay some eggs in the spring. The eggs should hatch into tiny fish in about a week. If you should notice some tiny transparent dots on the aquarium plants or in a nestlike hole in the bottom sand, you will know that they are goldfish eggs or minnow eggs. Observe some of them through your magnifying glass. You can look right inside the eggs and see the tiny fish developing. Many of the eggs will never hatch. But those that do may overcrowd your tank as they grow. Take out most of the baby fish. Start some new aquariums with them and give them as gifts to your friends.

Minnows are the only wild fish that can be raised with goldfish. The other kinds of fish that you can catch in ponds and streams are listed below. Some of the smallest of them can be kept in home aquariums, but not different kinds in the same tank or jar. Each kind needs its own private aquarium.

JOHNNY DARTERS. Darters belong to the perch family. They look somewhat like minnows and grow to be only three inches long. They are hard to catch because they dart away so quickly. They have two separate dorsal fins and very large front (pectoral) fins. They are usually greenish brown with black marks on backs and fins. There is also a rainbow darter, which is brightly colored. They live on the bottom of streams in shallow, cool water, where there are plenty of water weeds. They use their pectoral fins for climbing water plants and also to rest on as they lie on the bottom. Darters eat small water creatures and some algae. In an aquarium they will usually eat bits of raw meat.

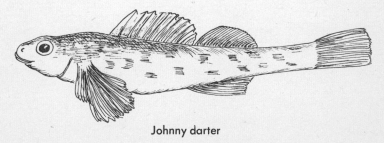

Johnny darter

SUNFISH. Young sunfish are colorful and can be kept in an aquarium. You can capture them in practically any pond or

lake in the country. They are short and flat, with rather round bodies. The dorsal fin is long with a very spiny front part. Since sunfish feed only on other living creatures, it is especially important to put them in a tank by themselves.

CATFISH or BULLHEADS. These are tough, smooth-skinned fish that live on the bottoms of ponds, lakes, and slow-moving streams. They are easily recognized by long whiskers, or barbels, around their mouths. The upper barbels help them sense what is happening above their heads while the lower barbels help in locating food. Both dorsal and pectoral fins have spines in them sharp enough to give you a nasty scratch if you are careless in handling a catfish. Young catfish under three inches long make good aquarium specimens. They eat both animal and vegetable foods.

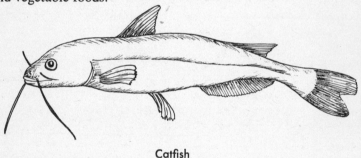

Catfish

SUCKERS. Suckers feed on the bottom of ponds and streams. They suck in their food with their round mouths, which are on the bottom part of their heads. Their mouths have thick lips that help them to suck in their food. Small suckers, not more

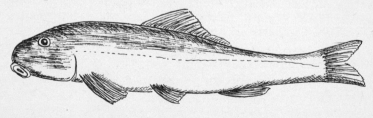

Sucker

than three or four inches long, can be kept in an aquarium. Feed them both animal and vegetable foods — bits of hamburgers, insects, cereal, ant eggs, dog food, etc. Have some mud on the bottom of the aquarium. The fish will suck their food from the mud bottom just as they do in their natural homes.

STICKLEBACKS. All sticklebacks have a row of sharp spines in front of the soft dorsal fin. Some have only three spines, others have five or ten. They are small fish, an inch and a half to three or four inches long when fully grown. At breeding time the male builds a nest of roots, algae, and leaves cemented together by a kind of glue made in the fish's body. The nest is shaped like a hut or an igloo and has at least one entrance hole. Several females lay their eggs in a single nest. The male then fertilizes the eggs and guards them till they hatch. Sticklebacks usually breed when they are about a year old and die before they are two years old. They make especially interesting aquarium specimens. Feed them tiny live water creatures (water fleas, worms, small insects, etc.) and bits of prepared fish food. Have plenty of growing plants in the aquarium, including at least one with a strong, upright stem. If you are lucky, one of your male sticklebacks will build a nest and attach it to the plant stem.

Sticklebacks are especially interesting to fish watchers because there are kinds that live only in fresh water, some that live in both fresh and salt water, and some that can live in salt water. Salt-water sticklebacks, like other marine fish, cannot be raised in a home aquarium because they need a constant renewal of sea water. A proper aquarium for ocean fish must have sea water piped in and out of it so that the water is always changing. This is a rather complicated project.

You can learn about some of the salt-water fish that visit or live in the shallow water and tide pools just by watching them. At low tide, watch for fish in places where they are likely to hide until the rising tide will again cover them with deep water. Here are some of the kinds of places to look for them: in puddles that are protected by large boulders; in rock pools with seaweed in them; in weedy rock crevices; and in the shallows among the sea grasses. In such places, depending on where you are, you are likely to see lumpsuckers, sea horses, pipefish, clingfish, flounders, toadfish, and other species that live close enough to shore to get caught when the tide goes out.

If you are a fisherman, in salt or fresh water, here is a way to make an interesting permanent collection that will show all of the different kinds of fish you catch. All you need for this project is some nondrying clay, plaster of Paris, cardboard boxes, water-color paints, plastic spray, and, of course, some fish. You will also have to have to have the use of a deep freezer or the freezing compartment in a refrigerator. Here are the steps to follow:

1. Catch a fish. Specimens that are six to eight inches long are best.
2. Put the fish into the freezer until it is frozen solid.
3. Put a layer of nondrying clay into the bottom of a cardboard box that is just large enough to hold the fish. Make the layer of clay a little more than half as high as the fish is thick.
4. Press the frozen fish into the soft clay. Press it down firmly until half of it is in the clay. Then remove the fish. You will have a clay mold of your specimen.

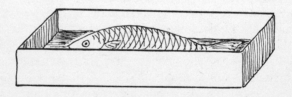

Press frozen fish into soft clay

5. In a clean tin coffee can, mix some plaster of Paris with enough water to make a paste as thick as evaporated milk.
6. Pour the plaster of Paris into the mold. Pour in enough to fill the hollow that was made by the frozen fish. Keep on pouring until you have the plaster of Paris at least one inch thick all around the fish model. Let it stand until the plaster is hard and dry. You should have a solid cast that is at least an

inch thick around the edges. This will make a thick, strong background for the raised mold of the fish.

Remove fish. Pour plaster of Paris

7. Lift the plaster cast out of the mold. To do this, you may have to peel off the edges of the cardboard box. Take the clay out and save it to use for another fish.

8. With a knife or a stick, clean off any bubbles or irregular bumps that may be on your cast.

9. Color the fish to look like the real specimen. Color the background sea blue or leave it white for contrast. If you do not have water-color paint, you can use chalk, pastels, or even crayons.

10. To preserve the colors, spray the entire cast with a clear plastic spray.

11. Scratch the name of the fish on the front of the cast or glue a label on the back showing the name of the fish and when and where you caught it.

12. Catch another kind of fish and follow the same steps.

By the method outlined above, you can make an accurate record of the fish you catch. A collection of fish molds can be made by several people working together. It is a good group project for showing the different kinds of fish that are available in any fishing area. Lifelike colored molds of fish are beautiful as well as interesting, for fish are among the most lovely of all living things.

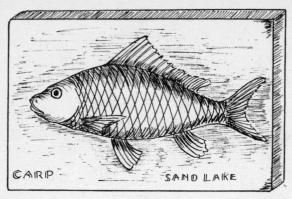

Finished cast

Man has always prized fish, which have provided him with food since prehistoric times. Today we still eat many kinds of fish, and the fishing industry is big business in most countries, including our own. As you know, fishing is a sport as well as a business. Many kinds of fish are protected by conservation laws. Therefore, before you collect or catch any fish, large or small, be sure that you are not breaking the game laws.

FIFTEEN

Seaweeds

Have you ever noticed patterns in the damp sand as the tide is going out? There are the holes and trails and burrows of crabs, worms, and other creatures that have hidden in the wet sand or scurried down to the surf. There are the starlike prints of the feet of sandpipers that run like lightning to the ruffled edge of a wave and then, just as swiftly, retreat from it. And there are the wavy lines and other rhythmical patterns made by seaweed as the ebbing tide drags it across the sand. Seaweed patterns look as though giant fingers had made long but delicate tracings in the sand.

As the tide goes out, it may leave piles of seaweed behind it. It is a common sight on most beaches to see huge tangles of drying seaweed recently cast up and left on the shore to die. A good way to find out about sea animals as well as about seaweed is to examine the next clump of seaweed you find on the beach. In it you may find such creatures as sea urchins, starfish, different kinds of gastropods, scallops, and hundreds of sand fleas. You are certain to find the interesting parts of the seaweed itself, which is one of the most unusual plants in the world.

Seaweeds are algae. They belong to the same plant group as the microscopic, one-cell diatoms, the slimy green pond scum, and the velvety fuzz that grows on the bottoms of boats. Algae are very simple plants and yet they exist in more forms than any other class of living things. In size, they range·from single-cell plants to giant kelps a hundred feet or more in length. They can live and grow in practically any kind of environment, on land, in fresh water, and in the sea. They vary in color from blue-green to golden brown. Knowing some of the facts about algae in general will help you to understand and enjoy the seaweed specimens you collect.

Algae, including seaweeds, have no true roots, leaves, or stems. Yet they do have special parts that do certain jobs. The most important job is the same for algae as for other kinds of plants. It is the changing of chemical material into living material. Animals cannot manufacture their own food. But most plants, using sunlight and a green material called chlorophyll, are able to make food out of the chemicals in air, soil, and water. Animals are completely dependent upon plants for food. The very tiny forms of marine algae are sometimes called "the grass of the sea" because they feed multitudes of animals that graze in the depths of the sea. Large forms of marine algae are the various kinds of seaweeds.

Most seaweeds grow attached to underwater rocks or other solid surfaces. The strands and clumps that are flung across the beach by waves and tide have been torn from their growing places. As you examine some seaweeds, you may see what appear to be plant roots. Seaweeds have no roots. Their root-like parts are *holdfasts,* which anchor the plants to rocks or other solid surfaces. Roots are tubes that bring food material to the plant. Holdfasts are merely anchors for holding the seaweed plant fast to a base.

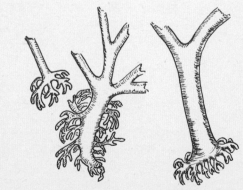

Holdfasts

Seaweeds have various methods of keeping afloat. Those that are lighter than salt water need no special aids. But the kinds that are made of heavy, dense material would sink and so grow downward away from the light if it were not for their air bladders, which keep them afloat. As you walk along the beach, look for seaweed that has tough little balloons of air. It is fun to step on them and hear them pop.

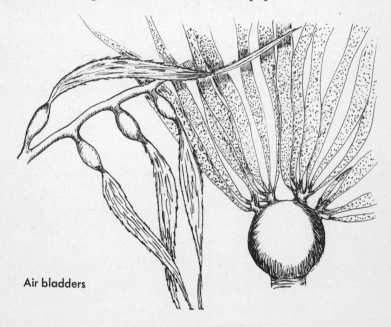

Air bladders

Seaweeds have no flowers and therefore no seeds. They reproduce more like animals than plants. Some seaweeds are male and some are female. Each kind of seaweed has special times of the year for reproduction. At such a time, some of the weed's tips become swollen as reproductive cells ripen inside. As soon as the cells are ripe, they ooze out in jelly-like masses. The tide mixes the male and female cells together in pairs. Each pair becomes a growing spore, which drifts away in the water until it settles on some solid surface. It then grows into an adult seaweed.

Scientists usually classify seaweeds in four main groups according to color: blue-green, green, brown, and red. In spite of differences in color, however, all seaweeds contain the green coloring matter, chlorophyll. In the case of red or brown species, other pigments are also contained, and these mask, or hide, the green.

If you want to find out firsthand about the kinds of seaweeds that grow in the waters off your shore, organize a seaweed hunt. Carry with you a pail or kettle with a handle, a spoon, and a strong jackknife. Later, you will need some large glass bottles or jars with good screw tops. The bottles in which freshly squeezed orange juice is sold in large food markets are excellent for preserving and exhibiting the different kinds of seaweeds and for making lovely seaweed gardens. Each time you discover a new kind of seaweed, cut off a typical piece of it or, if it is a small plant, scrape the whole plant off the base on which it is growing. Have your pail or kettle filled with sea water and just drop in each specimen as you collect it. You can study and separate and classify the specimens later. Try to get at least one sample of each of the four main groups of seaweeds.

Seaweed garden

BLUE-GREEN SEAWEEDS. Marine algae that are classified as blue-green are usually fuzzy or scummy, the kind of stuff that thrives in waters where nothing else can live. Look for *mermaid's hair* that lives on mud, rocks, and pilings in shallow water along the Atlantic and Pacific shores. This kind of algae consists of simple strands that are matted together. Look at the separate strands through your hand lens or through a low-power microscope. You may be able to detect the separate one-cell plants that are joined together to form the algae colony of which a strand is made. Blue-green algae have no special sex cells. They reproduce by splitting off cells to form new plants.

GREEN SEAWEED. Look for specimens of green seaweeds along the shore, especially if you live in a warm climate. They are often a delicate, pale green in color, and with silky, lacy, or ribbon-like blades. They reproduce by splitting off cells and also by means of sex cells. Green algae form the slippery scum that you find on wet rocks. When the algae dry out, they look like the lichens found in the woods. When they get wet again, they become slippery once more. Sea snails and other gastropods eat green algae from the rocks.

The largest of the green seaweeds is *sea lettuce*. It grows in shallow water and on rocks near shore. As its name suggests, sea lettuce often grows in wide green sheets or leaves. It may be as much as three feet long. *Codium* or *sponge seaweed* is

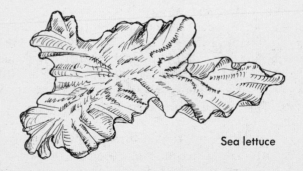

Sea lettuce

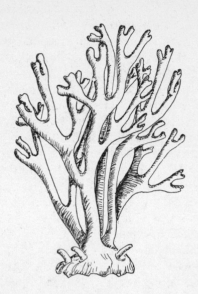

Codium

another common green variety found on both coasts. Each of its branching stalks branches into still more stalks until the whole plant looks like a river system and its tributaries. *Bryopsis* or *sea moss* is another branching kind of green algae. Its color is slightly darker than most green algae, and its branches are finer than those of the codium. Along the coasts of Florida and in other tropical waters there are many interesting green seaweeds. *Merman's shaving brush and mermaid's cup,* each looking quite like its name, grow on the floor of shallow areas.

BROWN SEAWEEDS. The great brown algae that grow in the seas are both interesting and important to man. Food, medicines, fertilizers, and other useful products are made from them. Brown algae contain a special pigment found only in these plants. This brown pigment covers up the green of the chlorophyll.

Probably the best known kind of brown seaweed is *fucus* or *rockweed*. It is found on all cool, rocky shores. You can recognize it, not only by its yellowish-brown color, but also by the air bladders that grow in its stems and strands. When a part

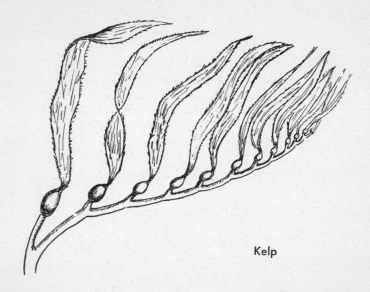

Kelp

of a fucus plant is broken off, it will keep right on growing and become a new plant.

On the Pacific Coast you can see great beds of *kelp*. Some of the individual plants grow to be a hundred feet long. The West Coast kelps are larger and more unusual than those on the East Coast. Kelps are greenish- or yellowish-brown, with holdfasts that attach them to rocks and air bladders that keep them afloat. Kelps of different kinds are often broken loose by the waves and tossed on the shore, where you should be able to find some specimens if you hunt for them. The largest of the Pacific kinds have long, slippery blades like ribbons, round air bladders, and a rubbery tube connecting the plant to its holdfast. The kelps of the Atlantic have blades that are wider and shaped like leaves or like long feathers or grouped together to form a many-fingered hand. In Ireland, kelp is collected from the rocky shores and burned to get out the iodine and other chemicals it contains.

The most famous of the brown seaweeds is *sargassum*, for which the Sargasso Sea was named. It is a floating plant, drifting for many miles in the warmer waters of the Atlantic and Pacific. Each sargassum plant resembles a land plant (except for its brown color). Its central stalk looks like a true stem, its blades look like leaves, and its clusters of air bladders look like fruit. This is only its outer appearance, however. It is a true member of the algae group and as such has no leaves, fruit, or true stems. Sargassum will make a good addition to your seaweed collection. It is delicate and attractive in its tree-like form.

Sargassum

RED SEAWEEDS. Seaweeds that belong to this group contain a red pigment that makes it possible for them to make food a hundred to two hundred feet below the surface, where some of the red species grow. Other kinds of red seaweeds are found in tide pools, where they often add a bright area of color and a delicate, graceful pattern. You may not be able to identify some of the typical "red" seaweeds because they may be green, purple-brown, or even reddish brown! Some of the red seaweeds are harvested for use in making chemicals and food.

Look for *dasya* among the rocks below the low-tide level. It is orange-brown to reddish purple, with tiny hairy branches, which give the plant a fernlike appearance when it is in the water. When it is removed from the water, dasya turns soft and slimy.

Irish moss is sometimes so dark in color that it looks purple with iridescent blue tones. Its thick, branched stalks look stubby and chopped off. Along the New England Coast it is gathered for the chemicals it contains. One of these, carrageenin, is used in making puddings, candy, and salad dressings. Look for specimens of Irish moss at low tide. It can be found among rocks above and just below the water's edge along the cooler northern beaches.

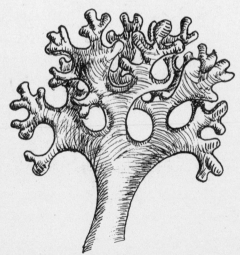

Irish moss

An interesting Pacific Coast seaweed is the *gigartina,* a thick, leathery plant found on rocks. It is harvested for its chemicals. Another important seaweed is *laver*, which is pink or red and shaped like delicate lettuce leaves. It is often used to make soup and is said to be delicious.

Corallines are red seaweeds that become encrusted with lime. This hardens the flat, wedge-shaped segments that make up the branches. Look for corallines in rock-lined tide pools. You will see some coralline seaweeds that are branched in a delicate, fernlike fashion. Others are mere crusts, like bright pink lichens, covering the rocks. When corallines are taken from the water and allowed to dry out in the sun, they become pure white. The corallines are among the most beautiful plants you can collect.

Corallina

As you look over the seaweed specimens you have gathered, you will notice how different they are in form, color, and texture. Yet they, and thousands of other large and small plants, are all algae. Therefore, if you want a name for your collection, you can label it MARINE ALGAE or SEAWEEDS. Both terms mean the same thing.

To preserve your collection permanently, float each flat specimen in a dishpan filled with water. (The three-dimensional, or nonflat, specimens will be handled differently later on.) Have ready a piece of fairly thick but soft white paper, larger than the specimen. Slip the paper into the water under the specimen. Arrange the branches or fronds in a lifelike pattern. Then lift the paper and the seaweed out of the water. Place on a pad of dry newspapers and allow the paper and the seaweed to dry slowly. Most specimens will stick to the paper as they dry. Add a label and, if you wish to protect the mount, cover the whole thing with cellophane or a heavier plastic.

Each of the thick, three-dimensional specimens should be put into its own exhibit jar. This can be any glass or transparent plastic jar that can be sealed shut. Place each specimen in a jar just large enough to hold it in a natural position. Then fill the jar with alcohol or with a 6 per cent solution of formaldehyde. An adult can buy either of these chemicals from a druggist. The chemical solution will preserve the seaweed almost indefinitely.

You can preserve your seaweed specimens for a long time in ordinary sea water. Fill your glass bottles and jars when you collect your seaweed. Then, make scientific exhibits by using a separate jar for each species (or each color family) of seaweed. For instance, one jar might hold samples of kelp or a single jar might be used for different kinds of red seaweed. Fill the specimen jars with sea water to the *very* top. Try to leave no room for even a bubble of air. Then screw the cap on as tight as possible. Turn the bottle or jar upside down to find out if it leaks. If it does, drip candle wax all around the edge of the cap.

In much the same way as described just above, you can make a beautiful undersea garden in practically any kind of large glass bottle. Fill it with sea water. Add strands of rockweed, air bladders with ribbon-like blades from kelp plants, a spray of sargassum, some feathery fronds of red coralline, or other interesting seaweeds. Then, drop in a rock or two that is encrusted with bright pink coralline, a few shells that have been thoroughly cleaned, a bit of driftwood, and a stone or two that has been sculptured by the waves. Do not crowd your sea garden. Have just enough kinds of things to make interesting, fluid scenes as you turn the bottle. Seaweeds, shells, and other treasures from the sea are interesting and artistic when they are kept in a setting of sea water. The water will not preserve the seaweed specimens, but it will keep them looking good for a long time.

SIXTEEN

Fresh-Water Plants

If you are exploring along the banks of ponds and streams, you can find samples of the kinds of algae that grow in fresh water. Fresh-water algae are smaller and far less numerous than the seaweeds that grow in the ocean. Other kinds of plants, however, are more typical of fresh-water banks and shores.

Fresh-water plants are simply the plant families that have adapted themselves to living completely or partly under water. As you observe them, you will discover that each has the same general features as plants that live on land. Some of their parts, however, are changed in order to make it possible for them to operate in a water environment.

A typical land plant has a stiff or woody stem to hold it upright; roots and rootlets containing hollow tubes that draw up food-bearing water from the soil; and solid leaves that grow upward toward the sun. A plant that grows entirely under water does not need to be held up by a stiff stem. It is held up by the water itself. Therefore, its central stem has become soft and flexible, moving gracefully with the motion of the water. Also, since a water plant is completely surrounded by water, typical roots are unnecessary. Hence, many water plants have no roots at all or roots that merely serve as anchors. The tissues of each plant's leaves and stems are able to absorb minerals directly from the water. The underwater leaves of water plants tend to be ribbon-like or divided into fine branchlets or delicate fringy leaflets. Water can easily flow through such feathery leaves without injuring them. Water plants with leaves that extend to the surface often grow floating pads that bob up and down in the water. But, except for some outward features that mark them as water dwellers, these plants are the same as land plants. They are typical of the flower-bearing plants that grow all over the earth.

In general, there are three zones of life for fresh-water plants: shallow water and shore for plants that have their roots under water and their stems, leaves, and flowers above; surface water for floating plants; and deep water for underwater plants that are attached to the bottom. In any typical pond in which plants grow, you should be able to find specimens from each of the three zones.

PLANTS IN SHALLOW WATER

CATTAILS are common plants that grow in swampy places and on the shores of lakes and ponds in most areas of the United States. They are tall and stiff, with strong central stems and tough leaves shaped like swords. The velvety brown "head" of a cattail is part of its flower. When the flower first develops, it is in two parts. The yellow top half is the male part. Below it is a green part, the female half. Insects, birds, and breezes carry pollen from the yellow part of one flower to the green part of another. Then the yellow part dries up, and the green part develops seeds. Each seed has a little parachute and is carried away by the wind. The green part of the cattail's flower turns brown by the end of summer, after its seed-producing job is finished. Cattails and other rushes are too large to be raised in aquarium water gardens but are most interesting to observe as the yellow and green flowers gradually change into fuzzy brown spikes.

BURREEDS are related to cattails. They have leaves like those of the iris family and round white flowers growing along their stems. The seed pods are round and covered with little spikes.

ARROWHEAD is another plant that holds its leaves above the water. The leaves are pointed and beautifully shaped like arrows. The delicate white flowers grow from a tall central stem. Arrowhead plants are greatly admired and are often planted around ornamental pools in gardens. They will grow in moist soil as well as in shallow water.

Most of the shallow-water plants are important to various

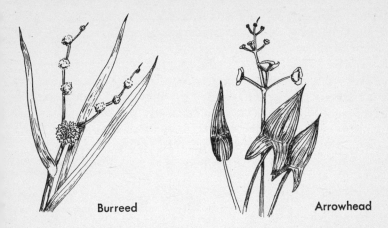

Burreed   Arrowhead

forms of life at the water's edge. The plants provide shade, shelter, and food for many insects, wild birds, and various kinds of water creatures.

WATER LILIES float their leaves and flowers on the surface, but have their roots in underwater mud. There are many kinds of water lilies. Yellow pond lilies, or spatterdocks, are common in most parts of the United States. Their globe-shaped, bright yellow flowers are favorite hiding places for insects. Look inside before you bury your nose in a spatterdock! White water lilies have large round leaves that lie flat on the water. The flowers are large, beautiful, and fragrant. The petals open when the sun shines and closes early in the afternoon. The American lotus has large dish-shaped leaves and large pale yellow flowers. Both the leaves and flowers are held slightly above the surface of the water. Their beautifully shaped, floating seed pods hold nutlike seeds, which are gathered and eaten by the Indians. Roots and young shoots are also used as food, not only by Indians and other human beings but by muskrats, too. The roots are as nourishing as potatoes.

PLANTS ON THE SURFACE

DUCKWEEDS are tiny plants that look like little green spots on the water. They float on quiet surfaces. All a duckweed plant really amounts to is a small flat leaf with a single threadlike root hanging below it. Some duckweeds have long, narrow leaves, some have round leaves, and some have two tiny leaves fastened together like a two-leafed clover. These little floating plants provide food for ducks and also for fish and other water creatures. Use a spoon or a jar to scoop up some water in which duckweeds are growing. They will grow well in your home aquarium, but do not let them get so thick that they completely cut off sunshine from underwater plants and animals. When this happens in a pond, many of the pond dwellers have to move elsewhere, and many of the underwater plants die.

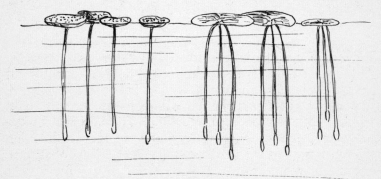

Duckweeds

WOLFFIA often grows among the duckweeds. It is the tiniest seed-bearing plant in the world. The whole plant is no bigger than the head of a pin! All summer long the tiny green wolffia plants manufacture and store up starches. By fall, each little plant is so full of starches that it sinks to the bottom. The water grows colder and colder, and winter comes. During the cold weather, wolffia plants live on the food that is stored in their tissues. By spring, the starch is used up and the plants are light enough to rise again to the surface.

PLANTS UNDER WATER

PONDWEEDS grow in such bunches that rowboats and small motor boats often have trouble moving through water in which they grow. There are several different kinds of pondweeds.

One kind has heart-shaped floating leaves on the surface and ribbon-like leaves under the water. Other kinds are entirely under water. Pondweeds serve as food for certain ducks, which will dive under water to bite off the juicy leaves. Insects and small fish are also found in areas where the pondweeds grow.

TAPE GRASS or EELGRASS has long and very narrow leaves rising from a cluster of roots. The slender, ribbon-like leaves wave gracefully with the motion of the water. Fish weave in and out among them. As you look down into a pond or a slow stream and watch the life and movement among the tape grasses, you will feel that you are looking into an underwater kingdom of silent motion, sun and shadow, and the blue, green, and silver of fish and plants.

Each tape grass plant is a cluster of stems, leaves, and roots. Runners go out from the base of the plant. Each runner starts a new plant. New plants also grow from seeds, which the tape grasses produce in a most unusual way. The plants have both male and female flowers. The male flower is a short-stemmed cluster that bears pollen. It grows under the water. When the

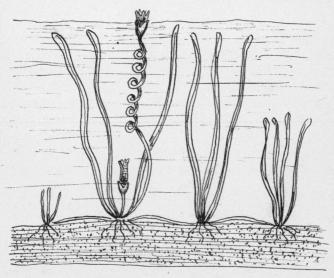

Tape grass

pollen is ripe, the flower breaks off and comes floating up to the surface. Meanwhile, the female flowers have been developing. These are delicate green blossoms that grow on long coiled stems. As the flowers ripen, the stems grow rapidly and uncoil enough to allow the blossoms to rise to the surface. When both male and female flowers are bobbing up and down on the surface, pollen is carried by water, wind, and insects. Soon the female flowers have all the pollen they need for making seeds. Their springlike stems slowly coil up again, pulling them back under the water, where the seeds develop, ripen, and finally scatter and grow into new plants.

BLADDERWORT is a rootless plant that lives under the surface. It provides a special kind of "shelter" for tiny water creatures. It eats them! It has a tangled mass of threadlike leaves that are divided like the limbs and branches of a tree. Small bladders are located in many of the forks of the branching leaves. These bladders are traps for catching food. As a tiny creature swims by, one of the bladders opens and sucks it in. Daphnia, cyclops, small mosquito larvae, and other tiny water animals are trapped and eaten.

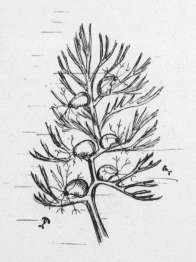

Bladderwort

Except for the carnivorous bladderwort, water plants are helpful and most important for fresh-water animal life. They add to the supply of oxygen. All gill breathers, as you know, depend upon oxygen in the water. Plants also offer shelter, resting places, and nests for water creatures. Many water insects, fish, amphibians, and other kinds of animals lay their eggs on or among the leaves and stems of water plants. Then, too, some plants supply food for the plant-eating or herbivorous water animals.

For any good fresh-water aquarium, you need some growing plants. Even though you may not want to raise fish, water insects, or any other kinds of water animals, you may enjoy raising water plants. A water garden can be a most graceful thing to watch and an interesting thing to study. And, unlike a rose garden, vegetable garden, or herb garden, a water garden can be made almost anywhere and will thrive in winter as well as in summer.

To make a water garden, begin with a large glass container — a big pickle jar, a wide-mouthed water bottle, a large refrigerator dish, a fish globe, or a regular aquarium tank. Cover the bottom with about two inches of sand or gravel that has been washed and washed in running water until it is completely clean. Fill with water from the pond or stream from which you are taking the plants. If this not convenient, use regular tap water and allow the filled aquarium to stand for about two days before you put in any plants. Letting the water stand in the air causes it to lose chlorine and absorb oxygen.

Put the rooted plants in place first, the tallest ones at the back of your water garden. Use some clean flat stones to anchor the sand or gravel around the roots. Put the shortest plants at the front. Arrange the plants so that different kinds of stems and leaves combine to make a delicate underwater scene. If you have any duckweeds or other floating plants, add them last to complete the garden.

To look its best, your water garden should stand where light can shine through the graceful plants. The direct rays of the sun, however, are likely to make the water become too warm and also to cause the algae to grow. This is especially true in the summer. If you place your garden in the full sun, you will soon have a smelly, soupy dark green mess, as the algae grow, die, and decay. The development of algae can be controlled by reducing the amount of sunlight and also by adding some algae-eating pond snails.

Once your water garden is well established, you may wish to add a fish or two. Fish and other gill breathers can help to balance your garden. They use up oxygen and give off carbon dioxide. The plants use up carbon dioxide and give off oxygen. A good water garden makes an ideal home for the right number of fish. To find out how many fish you should put in your water garden, you need to consider the amount of water in the container and the size of the fish. Then apply this formula, or rule: *For every inch of fish (not counting the tail) you need at least two quarts of water*. Hence, a one-gallon aquarium can safely hold *one* two-inch fish, OR *two* one-inch fish, OR *four* half-inch fish — plus their tails! You will find, however, that most fish will do better if they have more water and larger tanks than the limit given in the formula.

If you make a water garden and then add fish, you will have a bit of the water world to watch. Day-by-day observations of any tiny bit of living material, plant or animal, will help you to understand some of the scientific facts about life in general.

SEVENTEEN

Tide-Pool Exploring

Most people are fascinated by the sea and curious about the creatures that live in it. They enjoy finding out what life is like in the sunlit surface waters, in the green, shadowy depths, and in the valleys and caves of perpetual darkness on the ocean's floor. Passengers on glass-bottom boats, skin divers, and deep-sea divers enjoy the flashing colors of fish and other creatures, and the slow-motion rhythms of seaweeds. They see many sights that are strange and beautiful.

Beneath the surface of the sea there are animals that look like flowers, and darting flashes of bright-colored fish, and underwater gardens that grow in transparent waters, pale gold from the rays of the distant sun. Even in the cold, black depths of the sea where the sun never reaches, there are living things — fantastic fish that are different in shape, color, and habits from all the other animals in the world. In all areas of the sea there are creatures of strangeness and of breath-taking beauty. Many of them are seen and photographed by scientists who go down into the sea.

Probably you cannot go down into the ocean to observe the things that live and grow in its waters. But if you know how to explore a tide pool, you can make many discoveries about underwater life while you remain safe and fairly comfortable on land. You may have to lie head down and feet up for a while or stoop or squat against a rocky ledge or slip around a bit on some algae-covered stones. You will probably have to get your feet wet, and you may get a crick in your neck from holding your head in one position for a long time. But such discomforts will seem unimportant when compared with the thrill of discovery as you gaze into a tide pool and watch the beautiful and dramatic life below you.

Tide pools are found along any rocky seashore. When the tide is high, the pools and many of the rocks that protect them are covered with deep and often foaming water. Then, as the tide gradually goes out, much of the water leaves the tide pools, coursing and trickling out from among the rocks. Here and there, however, a sandy pool, a rocky basin, or a tight-walled corner in the rocks holds some water, even when the tide is at its lowest ebb. There are kinds of plants and animals that thrive in tide pools, where the water is sometimes deep and churning from the force of waves, and at other times shallow and so calm that it reflects fluffy white clouds drifting across a blue sky.

On some beaches the tide pools are a series of holes and pockets in and among the rocks, with each pool opening into another one. Here, inquisitive crabs and mollusk-hunting star-fish can move from pool to pool. There are other beaches where each tide pool is a separate body of water. The crea-tures that enter or leave it must do so by way of the land or by the sea itself at high tide. There are tide pools that are large and complicated in form, with caves and bays and islands and deep holes. And there are tide pools so small and simple that you can cross them in a single step and can see the entire sur-face in a single look. Large or small, a tide pool is a living community. Within it, life is supported by plants and animals living together and providing food for each other within their natural element, which is sea water. ·

When you go to the seashore, find a tide pool, settle down beside it, and explore its interesting inhabitants. Use your magnifying glass and examine every part, every rock, every living thing. How many of these things can you find in your tide pool?

Seaweeds, different colors and different forms
Mussels, scallops, clams and other bivalves
Periwinkles, whelks, limpets and other univalves
Sea urchins, green or purple
Chitons or their empty shells

Crabs, different kinds and sizes
Barnacles, acorn or gooseneck
Sea worms, soft ones and those with limy tubes
Sea anemones, and other flower-like creatures

Tide pool

You will probably not find *all* of these things in any one tide pool. But, if you keep on exploring, you will, in time, discover most of the things listed above. As you become an experienced explorer, you will learn not only *what* to look for but also *how* and *where* to look. You may be able to visit tide pools where it is easy to find most of the things listed above. You may also find many tide-pool creatures that are *not* listed above. There are sponges and corals and sea hares and jellyfish and a host of other interesting tide-pool inhabitants that can be found in certain coastal areas. A good observer makes many exciting discoveries in a pool where a casual looker sees only water, rocks, and sand. *You* are the explorer. What kinds of things grow in the tide pools you explore?

Notice the pieces of seaweeds that have been cast into the pool by the waves — red coralline or plumaria, or purple-red fronds of dasya, or slippery, branching brown rockweeds, or sheets or ribbons of light green sea lettuce, or some branching pieces of deep green codium. If your tide pool is in warm southern waters, look for the dainty mermaid's cup and the stiff merman's shaving brush.

Look for rocks that are covered with bright-colored scaly masses of algae. Even a very small rock may be a base or an anchor for some form of seaweed. With a short stick, touch the rocks and move the branches of seaweeds to discover what animals may be hiding there.

You may be lucky enough to discover some little scallops, which sometimes rest among the seaweeds. If so, watch them as they open their shells and allow the fringe of tentacles to wave in the water. Under these tentacles, their many bright blue eyes will be looking out for any sign of danger. Watch them as they flap their shells open and shut, seeming to take bites in the water as they move themselves forward.

Examine pockets in the rocks. In some of them you may find the spiny sea urchins, which have etched out the pockets for themselves. On the rocks' surfaces you may find layers and layers of acorn barnacles, so firmly attached that their shells have become part of the rocks. Here and there among the acorn barnacles you may notice colonies of gooseneck barnacles, with their tough but flexible stalks sticking out from the rocks.

Some of the rocks may be covered with layers of deep blue mussels, so closely packed together that each one is anchored to others beneath and around it. The mussels may be on the floor of your tide pool, too. You may find some empty mussel shells, clean and shining. Perhaps a hungry starfish forced them open and ate the soft flesh of the living mussels.

Watch for small starfish that may be prowling about on the

bottom in search of food. If you see one, notice the way it can move in any direction and yet never be going forward, backward, or sideward since it has no back or front, only a top and bottom. If you see a tangled mass of kelp or other seaweed, hunt through it for some of the starfish called brittle stars. They often cling to the seaweeds with their thin, prickly arms, which they coil and uncoil like the tentacles of an octopus. If you try to untangle one of these animals, it may break away from you by detaching itself from any tentacle you happen to hold. If this should happen, keep the disconnected tentacle to study through your hand lens. The brittle star will soon grow a new one for itself.

Turn over a few rocks and look for colonies of sea worms. You may find them in soft masses or in hard, shell-like spirals if they are tube worms. As you move a rock, you may uncover a crab, which will scamper off at once in search of a new hiding place. Hunt for different kinds of crabs among the rocks and seaweeds of the tide pool.

Univalve shells lie on the floor of most tide pools. Pick up some of them and examine them carefully. Some will be live shells, with the living animals safely tucked inside and sealed in by their operculums. Others will be the empty shells of dead snails. Still others will be the homes of shell-borrowing hermit crabs. Pick up one of these and watch the little hermit as it draws itself far back into the shell and attempts to cover the opening with its claws. Put it down again and watch it quietly until it peeks out to see if all is well.

Looking into some tide pools is like gazing down on a flower garden in full bloom. The sea "flowers" you are most likely to find in your tide pool are not really flowers at all. They are sea anemones, among the most beautiful and interesting of all tide-pool animals. You can find them on the Atlantic and the Pacific coasts.

Look for these soft-bodied little animals. They fasten the brown stalks of their bodies securely to rocks or sand. Each anemone has a crown of fleshy tentacles that wave in the water like the petals of an aster being blown by a breeze. The tentacles have stinging cells with which the anemone stuns its prey — small shrimps, fish, crabs, and the microscopic creatures of the sea. The tentacles draw the food to the mouth, which is in the center of the crown. After the anemone has digested the soft parts of its meal, it spits out the shells. Drop a tiny sea creature into the tentacles of an anemone and watch the eating process through your hand lens. Touch other anemones with your finger. At the touch, the tentacles will instantly be drawn in. What had been an open, waving crown of petals suddenly becomes a compact but soft ball, usually covered with grains of sand and bits of broken shells. This is the animal's way of protecting itself. It becomes a dull-looking bump on a rock or a sand-covered part of the pool's bottom.

Anemones are very simple animals. They have no bones, no shells, no brains, and no real sense organs, only a series of

Sea anemones

nerves, which are sensitive to light and touch. Like the fresh-water hydras, which you met in Chapter Five, they have a hollow tube for a stomach and a single opening (a mouth) to their bodies. But sea anemones have a special quality that delights all tide-pool viewers — color. Some are pink, some purple, some green, some cream-colored. Their colors are often brilliant, and a clump of anemones on an underwater rocky ledge looks like a bed of short-stemmed gay flowers. You will enjoy watching the anemones and touching them to see them draw themselves into a ball. But if you try to pry one loose, you will discover that it is almost impossible to do so without cutting or tearing the animal's base. And once out of water, anemones become limp and dull-looking. It is only in the water that they show their amazing beauty.

You may find some colonies of hydroids, which look like tiny anemones with pink centers. Their flower-like tentacles sway gracefully on the ends of tall stalks. They live and feed much as the anemones do. But they reproduce by budding, and the young hydroids grow either attached to or in a clump with the parent. This makes each hydroid family look like a many-stemmed plant, each stem crowned with a delicate flower. Clusters of tubularia, a kind of hydroid with a ring of short, petal-like tentacles on a delicate stalk, grow on rocks along the Atlantic Coast as well as in other parts of the world.

In pond water you can find a plant, the bladderwort, that eats meat as though it were an animal. And in tide pools you can find animals, the hydroids and sea anemones, that grow in fixed positions and have flower-like heads as though they were plants! Nature has created such a variety of living things that no one person can hope to see or understand all of them.

As you explore a tide pool, try not to disturb the life that is going on within it. Collect only the dead, empty shells that you find lying on the floor of the pool. They are like the bare bones left after a turkey dinner. The meat has already been eaten, and the hard parts have been discarded by the diners. Nothing will suffer if you remove the empty shells. But if you take some of the living plants and animals from the pool, nature's balance will be disturbed in the little community. Everything there provides food for something else. And for you, the tide pool is a window through which you can watch a small but living example of the graceful motions, the delicate beauty, and the endless eat-and-be-eaten life in the sea.

INDEX